Glenys Kinnock was born in 1944 in Roade, Northamptonshire. She is a teacher in a primary school in West London. She has had a lifelong involvement with the Labour Party, is a member of the board of UNICEF UK and chair of the management committee of One World Action, a third world development agency. She has been selected as Labour's prospective parliamentary candidate for south-east Wales in the European elections in June 1994. She edited the essay collection *Voices for One World* and her other books are *Eritrea – Images of War and Peace* and *Namibia – Birth of a Nation*. She married Neil Kinnock in 1967. They have two children.

Fiona Millar is a freelance journalist. She started her career as a graduate trainee with the Mirror Group, then spent eight years on the *Daily Express* as a news reporter, lobby correspondent, news desk executive and feature writer. She still contributes to the *Daily* and *Sunday Express* and writes the weekly political profiles in Parliament's *House Magazine*. She lives with political journalist Alastair Campbell in North London. They have two small sons.

The March of the Women

Shout, shout, up with your song!
Cry with the wind, for the dawn is breaking.
March, march, swing you along,
Wide blows our banner and hope is waking.
Song with its story, dreams with their glory,
Lo! they call and glad is their word.
Forward! hark how it swells,
Thunder of freedom, the voice of the Lord.

Long, long, we in the past,
Cowered in dread from the light of Heaven.
Strong, strong, stand we at last,
Fearless in faith and with sight new given.
Strength with its beauty, life with its duty,
(Hear the voice, oh, hear and obey),
These, these, beckon us on,
Open your eyes to the blaze of day!

Comrades, ye who have dared,
First in the battle to strive and sorrow.
Scorned, spurned, naught have you cared,
Raising your eyes to a wider morrow.
Ways that are weary, days that are dreary,
Toil and pain by faith ye have borne.
Hail, hail, victors we stand.
Wearing the wreath that the brave have worn!

Life, strife, these two are one!
Naught can ye win but by faith and daring.
On, on, that ye have done,
But for the work of today preparing.
Firm in reliance, launch a defiance,
(Laugh in hope, for sure is the end).
March, march, many as one,
Shoulder to shoulder and friend to friend.

Cicely Hamilton

Printed by kind permission of J. Curwen & Sons Ltd, London

BY FAITH AND DARING

*Interviews with
remarkable women*

**Glenys Kinnock and
Fiona Millar**

Published by VIRAGO PRESS Limited, September 1993
20–23 Mandela Street, Camden Town, London NW1 0HQ

A CIP catalogue record for this book
is available from the British Library

Typeset by Florencetype Ltd, Kewstoke, Avon
Printed in Great Britain by Cox and Wyman Ltd, Reading, Berkshire

Two remarkable women are sadly
missing from this book

– my dear brave friend, Jane Ewart Biggs,
who made such a difference to so
many lives

– and Aung San Suu Kyi, a woman of
immense courage and integrity who has
been held in complete isolation in her
home in Rangoon since July 1989

ACKNOWLEDGEMENTS

We are indebted and grateful to Ruth Petrie, our brilliant and supportive editor. We also wish to thank all the women we interviewed for the book who showed us such kindness, hospitality and patience. Most of all, thanks to Audrey Millar for transcribing endless hours of tape and Barbara Parry for her typing.

Last but not least, thanks to Neil and Alastair for their love and encouragement.

CONTENTS

GLENYS KINNOCK

Introduction
– 'By faith and daring'

This book is a celebration of women's lives and achievements. Each of the women interviewed in it is strong, resourceful and opinionated, and has made her mark on society. It was never our intention to focus on any one area of women's experience, so we have allowed them to speak for themselves, about their lives and work. Each one describes how she has worked for, or contributed to, change and faced challenges, success, satisfaction, frustration and disappointment along the way. They all believe in equality of choice and we often found our conversation turning to the need for freedom to be a working parent on an equal footing. The time has certainly come for flexibility, shared parenthood and shared responsibilities to move from rhetoric to realisation.

Although the interviews do represent the views and experiences of individuals, each of the women is a powerful advocate for her sex. Thoughts about the role of feminism today are a thread running through each contribution. There is a sense that women need to find ways to make their common interests and their collective power felt. We all know that, just at the moment we think battles have been won and much has been achieved, we are shaken out of our complacency by some blatantly misogynous act which reminds us to renew our activity. The price of progress, like that of liberty, is eternal vigilance.

There have been recent and important achievements for women

in Britain. The forthcoming ordination of women in the Church of England, the election of Betty Boothroyd as Speaker in the House of Commons and the verdicts in the High Court on the cases of women who lived lives of terror and who killed their husbands, are all forward strides in equality and justice. But the basic inequalities remain. Research repeatedly shows that women are more likely than men to be poor. Women remain disadvantaged socially, politically and economically – in their jobs, their homes and by the social security system. The assumptions made by society and its institutions are still founded upon the view that women are economically dependent on men. But the truth is that whether they live with men or not, thousands of British women are dependent on benefits which, rather than giving them a chance to get themselves out of poverty and debt, anchor them in both. The gap between women's and men's pay is wider in the UK than in any European country except Luxembourg. Five million women are part-time workers in jobs which usually deny them eligibility to sick pay, maternity pay, holiday pay and pension entitlement and they have fewer training and promotion opportunities. Only 35 per cent of women are in occupational pension schemes compared with 60 per cent of men. The state pension is a quarter of women's fulltime earnings and a substantive increase is needed to keep them out of poverty.

The consequences of poverty, unemployment and a society organised around market values and consumption have been deeply felt by thousands of families. Women's earnings are particularly affected by the abolition of the Wages Councils and by the lack of minimum wage arrangements of the kind which exist in all EC countries except Ireland. The increasingly fragmented collective bargaining structures also add to the disparities in earnings between women and men. Equal opportunity has to mean equal pay for equal work and we are a long way from achieving that. Lone mothers in Britain suffer particular hardships and face higher risks of poverty than lone fathers. A recent EC survey has suggested that the percentage of lone mothers in poverty was on average twice that of lone fathers.

More and more children are born and grow up in impoverished environments and many are being denied the chance to develop their full potential. Mothers on low incomes are subject to special pressures, to spend more than they can afford. The desire of many of the mothers of the children I teach, to ensure that 'the kids don't go short' makes them sitting targets for expensive credit – and the sharks know where to look for their prey. So many women feel that they have little prospect of escape from a life on an income which forbids the possibility of planning in the long term or thinking beyond the next meal, the next gas bill or the next pair of kids' trainers. One in five households is now headed by women, 70 per cent of them survive with only Income Support. Their lives are stressful, their self-esteem is low, and their prospects are grim. Women's poverty is intensified over a lifetime. They often cannot find money for day-to-day living and panic sets in when Christmas approaches or the need to buy a larger one-off item, like a cooker, arises. In households where the man is unemployed it is usually the woman who manages the finances and often bears the brunt of the stress and stigma associated with any debt which may occur.

In Britain over 60 per cent of male fulltime employees work over forty hours a week. These long hours which men work serves to reinforce the responsibility women have for childcare. The reality is that the lives of women everywhere are shaped by the traditional caring roles and responsibilities which they have. These roles determine and influence their lives, their aspirations and the decisions they take about jobs, work and so much else. The continuing presumption is that women simply do not need their own money or resources. A sense of dependency is frequently a feature within marriages and women develop a sense of powerlessness and insecurity. This is one of the main reasons for the breakup of relationships. Survey after survey continues to show that in practice the traditional division of labour within the home remains much the same. There is still a residual hostility to women working and the implication more often than not is that individual parents are totally responsible for their children. The view of a traditional pattern of life, that in reality only the wealthiest can sustain, remains.

It goes back again and again to women's invisibility. Much of the research and the statistics which emerge make sweeping generalised and outdated assumptions about family structures. Little account is taken of the effects of poverty beyond its definition as a shortage of material resources. Women living on low incomes have a sense of being marginalised and isolated. There is talk now of the 'feminisation of poverty' and this I welcome since it is at last a recognition of the increasing visibility of the vulnerability of women's poverty whether they live alone, as a lone parent, as an elderly pensioner or within a family with a partner. There is increasing recognition that government policies now and in the last decade have been driven by a powerful, determined ideological engine. The decrease in public provision of services, the harking back to family responsibilities and the deregulation of the labour market have hit women hardest of all. More and more women are caring for elderly dependent relatives whose needs are not being met by the state. They continue to be denied the level of financial recognition justified by the role they play as carers. Women carers are also losing out on careers and on their ability to make provision for their own retirement. The government's 'front line providers of social care' policies fall heavily on women. Similarly women's full maternity rights are being denied in Britain. In line with the root and branch objection to European-wide standards for social provision, the government obstructed the European Pregnancy Directive. They delayed it and diluted it. One in five pregnant women in Britain has no right to maternity pay at all and virtually no part-time workers will see any improvement in maternity pay. Maternity benefits will be related to sick pay provision. That makes Britain the only country which treats pregnancy as an illness. Eligibility conditions exclude many women in Britain from the maternity leave which is a universal right for employed women in all EC countries.

Many of these issues are a far cry from much of the discussion currently taking place about feminism, 'post-feminism' and 'the backlash'. They are, however, increasingly the subjects raised by all those who see the necessity of finding political solutions to the inequalities in our society. Increasingly the view is that women's poverty, the stress within families and the increased divorce rate make life especially tough for women. Also it is clear that our campaigns have to be about working for changes which lead to economic self-sufficiency and self-empowerment. Government policies must respond to changing patterns of family life and should learn from some of our European partners about social policies which promote equality. Women on current trends are likely to remain low paid and segregated in the work-force. We need minimum wage law and more and better education and training for skilled workers across the labour-force – and not just in what is regarded as traditionally women's work. Research into the economics of equal value shows that job segregation between men's work and women's work remains one of the biggest causes of average female pay being about 70 per cent that of males.

The Equal Opportunities Commission has already challenged the myth that the British economy cannot afford to pay women a fair wage. There are naturally implications for labour costs but the assumption that the economy cannot afford it emphasises labour costs while playing down the comparable advantages of productivity and sheer human development and opportunity. In this as in so many other areas it is an uphill struggle to challenge the discrimination based on historical views of women's position in our society.

There has been a lot of talk about a 'glass ceiling' that women hit because of lack of access to childcare, decent maternity leave and pay disparities. There remains no commitment to legislation which would enable more women to effectively challenge the traditional male hierarchies in the professions. Anti-discrimination laws need to be underpinned as it is not enough to rely on voluntary action from companies and/or market forces. Conscious as we are about the much discussed backlash it should still be recognised that the balance of discriminatory forces at present works against women. Opponents of positive action often use the argument about merit to justify a position which denies the fact that discrimination exists on a scale which excludes women from real equality. In the USA companies have 'diversity' programmes governing the promotion of women – the government decision on bids for contracts has to take a company's policy on the employment of women and ethnic minorities into account. In America as well as Europe employers now recognise that as the birth rate has fallen so access to jobs for women has to increase. This happened in the 1950s and opportunities increased and wages for women improved. If we recognise this then we must identify the barriers women face which have absolutely nothing to do with their ability and talent. Education and employment opportunities must catch up with the changes which our society has experienced.

The government initiative called Opportunity 2000 is a boardroom based campaign which has been an effective PR exercise for them and for a few large companies and has done nothing for the medium and small businesses where most women work. The government should look to its own back yard and to the fact that in some departments there are no women in the top three grades such as the Inland Revenue where 60 per cent of the staff are women. Here, as elsewhere, women feel that in large organisations people have an innate tendency to hire and promote those who resemble themselves. One owner said, 'Our managers are all white, middle-aged men and they appoint in their own image'. Women are too often self-effacing, lacking in confidence and unwilling to express their views as forcefully as men. People marvelled at Mrs Thatcher because she so obviously failed to conform to this stereotype. This is changing slowly but it points to the need for more awareness of the conditioning which can lead women to feel uncomfortable and out of place in positions of power.

Investment in decent, affordable childcare has to be central to the achievement of our goals. Let's face it – two thousand Opportunity 2000 initiatives will not bring change until we have gained this crucial provision. Policies which make it easier for women and men to happily combine family responsibilities and work makes sense for them and for the economy.

In this, as in so many other spheres of social policy, we see the application of Thatcherite principles. The government still intends to get childcare on the cheap and there is little recognition of the fact that it is those who can least afford to pay for care who most need to go out to work. The traditional ideology of the right is that a woman belongs in the home and that the state should not take on what are seen as parental responsibilities. These views do not take into account the fact that mothers of young children are playing an increasingly important role in the workplace, even in the recession. It is therefore alarming to realise that the quantity and quality of organised childcare in Britain is lower than in any other European country except Portugal. The UK provides the second lowest level of daycare facilities for children aged from three to school age, according to a recent Equal Opportunities Commission report. The experience of what is possible is so limited in the UK that the problem is not properly addressed. At the last election, the Labour Party had a commitment to the expansion of the provision of child-care so that families had a choice which matched their needs. Investment in the development of a partnership between the public, voluntary and private sectors would have offered diversity and real choice for parents.

The economic advantages of greater public investment in pre-school and after-school care have been strongly presented by the Institute for Public Policy Research. They have argued that the costs to the state would be offset by the increased tax paid by mothers on higher earnings. Similar advantages would accrue from offering childcare opportunities to women who want to go to work but are forced to live on benefits.

Childcare remains a major barrier to the achievement of real equality of opportunity because it naturally inhibits their access to training and employment. It was an issue which, incidentally, did not receive even a passing mention by the prime minister when he made a lengthy speech to launch Opportunity 2000. The government's approach is, as always, governed by the view that the family should function as a private unit which does not depend upon public provision – an approach that has more in common with pre-Clinton USA than with our European neighbours. But with one important difference – parents in the USA can offset a proportion of childcare costs against their income tax. The

European Commission notes that the UK and Ireland are alone in largely targeting public provision to 'at risk' children and not at the more general needs of the children of working parents.

It is important to note that increasingly the argument is being made for a rethink of the current concentration on campaigns for the national provision of childcare. We need discussion now about the need for increased flexibility in working hours and for greater co-operation between parents in the upbringing of their children. It is time we stopped labelling childcare as a mother's problem. No amount of legislation will take away the guilt women feel about going out to work, or indeed compensate them for the dual roles they play. However, if their skills and talents are not to be wasted we need fundamental changes in working patterns.

Only one in three British employees now works a standard 9–5, Monday to Friday. By the year 2000 half the work-force will be women and some companies are already recognising the need for greater flexibility – in the interest of their employees but also in the interests of productivity and profits. It is time we questioned the assumption that women want the same fixed working patterns as men or that they necessarily *want* fulltime childcare. Women with young children often prefer part-time working but find that this can mean losing out on pay and promotion. This has to change and surely it should when employers already recognise the commitment they get from their part-timers. Provided fundamental changes can take place in the attitude to giving responsibility and status to part-time workers, this could be one of the ways forward for parents who simply want more time with their children.

Meanwhile many women advance their careers at considerable personal cost and there is evidence that they suffer greater stress than their male colleagues. An Institute of Directors survey has shown that 43 per cent of female directors are childless. This contrasts with 92 per cent of male managers who are married and 86 per cent with children.

The old boys' network is alive and well in the workplace and it is clear that senior managers' attitudes to women's employment are changing more slowly than corporate image-makers and government ministers like Gillian Shephard would have us believe. Of the thousands of directors on the boards of Britain's biggest 100 companies, thirty are female and twenty-six of these are non-executive. In 1992 the NHS, Europe's largest employer of women with 780,000 female staff, 79 per cent of its total, had only 18 per cent top women managers. There have been commitments to change but, as the Royal College of Nursing points out, the key issues of low pay, training and maternity provision are not being addressed. In the Civil Service women make up nearly half of the work-force but only 8 per cent are in the top three grades. Only three out of eighty-three High Court judges are women. Women occupy only 3 per cent of university professorships and lecture-ships and 18 per cent of medical consultants posts. Only 8 per cent of architects are women, 10 per cent of chartered accountants, and 10 per cent of local government managers. Men are 50 per cent more likely than women to be offered job-related training. The proportion of women in the House of Commons is still only 9 per cent. Only Ireland, France and Greece have lower percentages of women MPs. The rise in the 1992 general election was almost entirely due to the increase of Labour women MPs from twenty-four to thirty-seven. Only twelve of the UK's eighty-one Members of the European Parliament elected in 1989 were women.

There is clearly a need to increase our understanding of the issues that affect women. Our aim should be to change attitudes, strengthen women's sense of their own worth and campaign for legislation to promote equal opportunities. The social and political climate is ripe for change. It is not a case of special pleading on behalf of women but rather of a recognition that so many aspects in our society are impoverished because a large section of the popula-tion is not playing its full part.

In Europe, particularly northern Europe, images of family life and family structures have changed radically. There, changes are a reflection of the changes experienced by women. In Ibsen's *The Doll's House* (1879) Torvald says to Nora, 'Before everything else you are a wife and mother'. She replies, 'I don't believe that any longer. I believe that before everything else I'm a human being –

just as much as you are.' These are powerful words which still have a resonance for us today.

We should not be deceived, however, by the window dressing of those who flaunt images of success and achievement as evidence that we live in post-feminist times – films and advertising full of dynamic executive women who manage a baby and a home too! The reality is far removed from the image. There is still an insidious conditioning which leads young women to avoid science and engineering degrees and towards low paid, low status jobs. A woman's guilt about parenting grows in a climate which asks more and more of her. While opportunities to work outside the home have improved, so have obligations within the home. She listens to young children read, she helps with GCSE assignments and she cares for the child's physical well-being, and any shortcomings in any of these areas are seen as her failure since the responsibilities are 'naturally' hers. Maternal responsibilities can be onerous and they continue to grow. Young girls can now see the possibilities but their gaze is distracted by the unreal world on offer in television soaps – a world which does not prepare them for the challenges they must meet and face.

Since I first grappled with these ideas in the 1960s and early 1970s, and developed them alongside my socialism, there has been remarkable progress and feminists continue to work for radical change. At that time domestic violence and sexual harassment were unmentioned aspects of women's lives. Women did not have enough *gravitas* to read the news on television. Women did not receive the same pension payments as men, they had no right to equal pay for equal work and there was no legal entitlement to maternity pay. Teachers routinely treated boys and girls differently – they lined up separately, they played different games and read books which clearly predicted their future stereotyped roles. There was little questioning twenty years ago of the domestic responsibilities women should shoulder. There were few rape crisis centres or refuges for battered women. We were a million miles away from believing that a woman could be prime minister or ordained into the Church of England or defeat the antiquated structures of the judiciary. There are signs now too that women are offering a critique of political culture which cannot be ignored. During the last two decades women have worked for radical social change and for social solutions. Triumphalism would be inappropriate, but we need to celebrate significant advances.

As we mark up what has been achieved and ponder how we network, lobby and campaign for further change, we must also recognise the need to explore the lives of women in a wide and diverse world. In my contact with women who live in the South, I have learned that you cannot presume that we have a global community. The UN quote is still relevant: 'Women constitute half of the world's population, perform nearly two-thirds of its working hours, receive one-tenth of the world's income and own less than one-hundredth of the world's property.' Religions and ideological fundamentalism oppress women and deny them the right to their choice of education, healthcare and lifestyle. Out of 100 million children not in primary school, two-thirds are girls who are being robbed of their childhood, working in and outside the home. The World Health Organisation estimates that 90 million girls and women alive today have been subjected to genital mutilation. In Kuwait, women are not even allowed to vote.

These are only a few of the appalling facts which have led to UNICEF asserting that a new world order should oppose the apartheid of gender as vigorously as the apartheid of race. The reality is that everywhere in the developing world – from the urban slums and shanties to the impoverished rural communities – women will be working from dawn until dusk for little reward or recognition.

I have been trying to describe the case for women to exercise rights commensurate with their extensive responsibilities. The truth is that on almost any scale of measurement, and in almost any situation, women contribute most. And within the global generalisations, there are huge disparities that show the intensity of disadvantage suffered by women.

These, and many other concerns, are reflected in the words of the women in this book. There is, I believe, a positive message contained in their words and in their accomplishments. They represent many thousands of women whose praises go unsung and I salute them all for being generous, courageous and indomitable fighters for change.

Mary Wollstonecroft said: 'It is justice, not charity, that is wanting in the world.' Her words, written two hundred years ago, have a modern ring as they make the connection between women's rights and making a society as a whole more equitable. Now is the time to mobilise the precious sense of what is possible for women everywhere.

BETTY BOOTHROYD

'Out of the womb into the Labour movement'

Betty Boothroyd, the MP for West Bromwich West, is the first woman Speaker of the House of Commons.

I was an only child born of textile workers in the West Riding of Yorkshire. Both my parents were in the textile union and in the Labour Party at a very local level, so I came out of the womb, if you like, into the Labour movement. My father was in his mid-forties by the time I was born and never expected to have a child so I was very protected by him. Even when I was a young girl and going to youth clubs, he would come and collect me. I was never allowed to come home on my own. Although he died when I was eighteen he had a great influence on my early life in terms of his discipline, his ideas, his ideals, the way he felt people should behave in society and the way he thought they should behave towards each other. I suppose I was a bit of a rebel and stood out against authority in school and he always taught me to stand up for myself. I was born in Dewsbury with dark satanic mills and not very good housing conditions around me, and when you are born in those circumstances you want to make changes and to improve people's quality of life. He was always striving for that.

We were a poor family, but we had very high standards. My father always hung his clothes up on coat hangers and brushed his coat collars every night, he took care of his clothes and his shoes were always stuffed with newspaper to keep them in shape. He used to go to the market every Saturday to buy bits of leather to repair our shoes on Sunday. I don't repair my shoes, but to this day I still stuff my shoes with tissue paper. We didn't have very much, but what we had was always very well taken care of. That was the type of discipline that I grew up with.

I remember periods before the war, when my father was unemployed, when we used to pray in the winter for snow so that on the Monday morning he could go down to the council offices and get a job shovelling snow. My mother worked as a weaver, apart from a few weeks off when I was born, until she was sixty-five. She used to say: 'I'm not employed for my sex appeal, I'm employed because my rate of pay is lower than your father's.'

I can still remember the injustice towards those women who arrived at the mill a few minutes late for their early morning shift to find the door shut firmly against them so they had to wait outside until eight o'clock, when the workers got their first break, to get inside. I have never used the word 'feminist' to describe myself but I have lived my life by those principles. I was brought up by a working mother and grew up in a household in which the woman worked and kept the family together. My grandmother used to look after me while my mother was at work. I went to school with the local kids in the street then came home at dinner time with my grandma and went back to her at four o'clock. There was no great soul-searching about it and I don't feel I missed out, because when my mother was there, there was so much. We used to sit by the fire and switch the lights off to save a bit of money, and just talk. Even today I always switch lights off when I go out of rooms. Right up until she died, my mother used to look if there were any lights on in my room and say: 'This place looks like the Blackpool Illuminations.'

The happiest day of my parents' life was when I got a scholarship to the local technical college. It meant I would be doing subjects like English, English literature, French, book-keeping, shorthand, typing and grammar; all the things which would help me earn a better living than they had ever had. On one occasion I had an accident and had to have a couple of weeks off school, which was my idea of heaven, but my father walked to school every day during his dinner break to get my homework. I had a very happy childhood. I never really worried about not having brothers or sisters. I was so happy and content in that environment. Of course my father's death came as a great shock because, although he had been ill for a long time before he died, I was young and thought he would recover and then I was left without this tremendous figure in my life.

My first ambition was to be a window dresser. I used to love walking around Dewsbury and looking in shop windows. There was one particular shop which was full of wonderful things like whalebone corsets, pins and needles and haberdashery. By the time I went to the technical college, the height of my ambition was to work in an office and later to be a dancer. My father thought that I could work in the local town hall, in the rating department, which would offer me greater security than either of my parents had in their wildest dreams. As it turned out, my first job was in a department store, a very posh one in Dewsbury which we could never afford to shop in ourselves, so it was wonderful to be able to go to work there. My weekly wage was £1 a week and in the first week I got a 50 per cent increase.

Although we were a poor family, what little extra we had was devoted to me and I always went to dancing classes. We used to belong to the Co-operative Society and I still remember the number 12249 because we bought everything there and the dividend was always saved for me, for my dancing and for any equipment that I wanted. I loved to dance; I loved the music and the movement and, for a time, that was what I wanted to be. My father didn't want me to go away from home and it broke his heart when I did go, at seventeen. My mother, who was rather more indulgent, obviously realised it was better for me to get it out of my system, so in that terrible winter of 1947 I left home and went to dance at the Palladium and at Luton. It came to an end because I had a nail in my shoe of which I wasn't aware, which gave me a very bad foot. I also hated being away from home and they missed me so much that I just packed it in after a year. It is an episode in my life which, since then, has been blown up out of all proportion.

The politics started when I joined the Labour Party League of Youth at sixteen. I was on the National Consultative Committee and won two national public speaking contests in the Labour Party as well as being an agent in two parliamentary elections. I was then in my early twenties and not thinking of becoming an MP. I always saw myself as the secretary or the agent – the power behind the throne – because I was a woman and I thought that was the be-all and end-all for women.

Then I heard of a secretarial job going at Transport House in the research department. I knew about it because I came up to London for monthly meetings of the National Consultative Committee. My father had passed away by then and I hated leaving my mother, but she never stood in my way. She knew that it was very much in my blood and that I was hemmed in in a small town. After I left, I always went home at weekends to see her.

Then I moved over to the House of Commons to be a shared secretary to the MPs Barbara Castle and Geoffrey de Freitas. Working here was beyond my wildest dreams, but then I started to think: 'Well I could do this job too.' I wasn't in awe, I knew that I too could help to make changes. However at that time it was terribly difficult for a woman to get selected. In 1957 I wanted to be considered for an unwinnable seat and I went to see the then general secretary of the Labour Party who said: 'Eeh lass, don't just sit there looking at me with those big brown eyes, you want to go off and get some age on your shoulders first.' At the time the Tories were bringing all their young people in and I thought: 'Damn you, I am going to do it anyway.' So when Captain Waterhouse, the leader of the Suez rebels, resigned from South East Leicester, I went up there and got selected. I was the only person who thought I could win that seat with a 21,000 Tory majority! I then went on to fight Peterborough, Nelson and Colne in a by-election and Rossendale. I was finally successful on my fifth try – a by-election in West Bromwich in 1973. Most people might have given up by then but I was determined and I am terribly resilient. I really did get where I am by faith and daring – faith that one day I would get into Parliament and daring to run against the establishment. My desire to get here was like miners' coal dust, it was under my fingertips and I couldn't scrub it out.

I got tremendous encouragement from men back then, but, I am sorry to say, not from women. I never once got a nomination from a women's section – they tended to go for the nice-looking young man rather than the woman – and when I was finally selected for West Bromwich, I was accused by one woman of not being married, not having any children and not having had a hard life washing nappies or doing the shopping. I don't think it goes on quite like that now but it is still hard for women because they are often accused of not having had a family, but if you do have one they want to know how you are going to look after them – the sort of question they never ask of a man. If I had married, I doubt I would have become Speaker.

It is also difficult for women when they get here because they are expected to do everything plus the women's issues and the hours are very difficult for anyone with a family. The Labour Minister Judith Hart once said, in a debate with Mrs Thatcher: 'You either have to have a gem of a granny or enough money for a nanny.' Judith had the granny and Thatcher had the nanny and if women want to come here, they have to have someone else at home to take their place. I hope the fact that I have broken through into this male stronghold will be an example to other women. I am very impressed by those who have come in here recently; the way they get up and challenge and ask questions and seek adjournment debates and never give up.

My mum was still alive when I got in and she was as proud as punch and was always with me. I remember once in West Bromwich, when I had the biggest majority I ever got, but I thought I was going to lose and was in a terrible panic, she said to me: 'If you lose you're still my daughter.' Those are the sort of crazy things that mothers say; of course I knew I would still be her daughter, but I'll never forget it. She always kept my feet on the ground while enjoying my success. Getting here was the height of my ambition and I always wanted to be a good constituency MP. The interests of my constituents in the Black Country towns were very similar to the interests of the West Riding of Yorkshire. Both areas are populated by hard-working people in dirty industries with low wages, so their interests were also ingrained under my finger-nails.

I was made a Whip in government in 1974. When the Chief Whip phoned me up to ask me if I would do it, I said I felt I wasn't really established enough as I had hardly made any speeches, to which he replied: 'Oh, keep your trap shut girl and you'll get on.' To some extent he was right. I then went to the European Parliament in the first group until 1979. I have always considered myself in the centre in party terms, because that is what the people of this country want. They don't want massive changes, they want things done their way. But even when the party went through a very difficult period, it never occurred to me to leave. When the SDP was founded, one or two people came to see me and argued that I should go but there was no way I would leave the Labour Party. Everything I owe is to the Labour Party and I believe you should stay and fight for what you want.

It is in my nature never to give up and I have got where I am by the inevitability of gradualness. I kept trying to get on the National Executive Committee and eventually did so when Shirley Williams left for the SDP and I had been her runner-up. I left the NEC when I was put forward by my party as Deputy Speaker after being on the Speaker's Panel of Chairmen for a long time. Becoming Speaker wasn't something I had thought of doing, but then I never analyse myself. I just take everything in my stride. I am not a fixer in any way. Of course, once I became Deputy Speaker, I thought the Speakership might come my way so I had to be prepared. But it wasn't until after this last election that I thought it could become a reality and then I thought: 'By God, go for gold Betty.'

I have been stretched and it has been hard work but I have enjoyed every minute of the job so far. Ours is an adversarial and robust

House. People come here to change the flow of the Thames, to make change in our society, and therefore one has to expect robust behaviour, which I enjoy. What I do not want is for us to lose our traditional common courtesies here. By all means let us have robust argument, but good temper costs nothing. I would like to go down in history as a good, fair and just Speaker but no one is ever going to say that while I am in that chair. They will only say it when my toes are turned up. I can only be myself and people can't try and mould me. I couldn't wear the wig. I have never tried on a full bottomed wig, but I just looked at it and, although I am a traditionalist and wear robes that befit the job, I knew I couldn't wear a wig because I have to be comfortable.

My mother died in 1982 and that was one of the two things which brought tears to my eyes after I was elected Speaker. She was with me all my life and gave me support in everything I did and I only wish she could have known about this. The other occasion which brought a drop to my eye was being taken out into the yard and hearing the bells of Westminster Abbey ring out to welcome the new Speaker on the day after I was elected. It is an isolating job. I miss the camaraderie of my colleagues and going into the tea room and grabbing a cup of tea and having a chat. I can't do that now – by tradition the Speaker doesn't do those things – and although I have a terrace of my own here, I look out of the window a bit longingly on a nice evening. I am never lonely though. To miss people is one thing but to feel loneliness is quite another and God has blessed me in that I have never known what loneliness is all about.

MARGARET SIMEY

*'Injustice has made
me an angry woman
all my life'*

*Margaret Simey has lived and worked in the Toxteth area of
Liverpool for most of her adult life. She served for over twenty years
as a councillor and from 1981 to 1986 she was chair of the Merseyside
Police Authority.*

My father was a Glaswegian who became a clerk to the magistrates'
courts in the Gorbals and developed an acute social conscience. I
don't ever remember not being in an angry household. We moved
to Liverpool when he got a job there as principal of a college at the
end of the First World War. Until then I had been cocooned in St
Paul's Girls School in London, where we played cricket rather than
tennis. It might as well have been a convent; there was never a male
in sight. I opted out and left without any bits of paper because I
wasn't interested in becoming a top civil servant – the height of
female ambition in those days. I wanted to be either a lawyer like
my father or a doctor, but the obstacles for a woman defeated me.

I can still remember the night we left London for Liverpool,
early in the twenties. It was dark and as we crossed the Runcorn
Bridge over all the great mud flats of the Mersey, the chemical
works suddenly blew, the way they used to do, and the furnaces
blazed up. And the smell of rotten eggs! Even then, straight out of
school, I remember gulping with excitement and saying, 'This is
for real. This is it.'

I lost my heart to Liverpool immediately. We had a house in a decrepit Regency watering place on the river front where we could watch all the ships going up and down. I was lucky that it was assumed that I would have as good an education as my brothers so I went to Liverpool University. Because I liked the ships, I decided to do geography, but in the middle of my first year it was announced that a Charles Booth Memorial Chair had been created by the university. The new professor said that his main interest would be the study of society. That rang such a bell in my mind that without consulting anybody – parents had to pay in those days – off I went to become his first student.

Right from the start we were taught that it was the society rather than the individual that really mattered. Of course Liverpool is superb material for that because it is such a mix of nationalities and cultures, all stirred in a pot together. It wasn't a stable society, simply a melting pot of humanity. I saw myself as a student of society. I was never interested in doing good to individuals. I used to go to girls' clubs down by the docks simply because that was the only place where I could get any square dancing or folk dancing. The Victoria Settlement happened to be the stalking ground for emancipated women in Liverpool so I fell into their clutches and met Eleanor Rathbone [an independent MP and suffragette who persuaded the House of Commons to accept family allowance for women].

Eleanor never spelled out just why she was so passionate about equality – she was a doer not a talker – but I think the clue is that she studied philosophy at Oxford under the great Scottish moral philosopher Edward Caird. He argued that everybody, including women, had an equal right to try to fulfil their own destiny, to be themselves. That meant that you had not only a right to be yourself but a right to be a member of the society you lived in. The vote was the symbol of the fact that women were denied the right to be equal citizens. That was 'the cause' we were all committed to. It was the injustice of denying Jews or black people or women their right to belong to the community, to be equal citizens, that has made me an angry woman all my life. I am a 'socialist', not an individualist.

It was that first generation of emancipated women who really invented social work as a profession. When the men came back after the First War, they took their jobs back. Women were desperate for work so they turned the charitable jobs they had always done into a paid profession. That wasn't men's work so women could say, 'This is our territory. Here we have priority.' Eleanor was the moving spirit behind setting up the School of Social Work so that women could be properly trained. I was in fact the first ever student to take a degree in social science.

They were wonderful inspiring times for a young woman like me, and immense fun, in spite of all the poverty around us. To meet the first local woman barrister and the first policewoman – a voluntary service then – was a revelation of what women could do. They felt they had an obligation to train us younger ones. The Women Citizens Association, now the Townswomen's Guilds, was started to teach us how to use the vote once we got it.

We wanted equality for a purpose, not just to get jobs for ourselves. We were in this world to make it a better place and we couldn't do that unless we had equal rights as citizens. I would look at my brothers who weren't half as pushy as me, and think, 'Why can they get up in church and read the Bible and I can't?' I remember that when we got the vote, they threw a great public dinner in Liverpool. Afterwards, I couldn't understand why the streets were dancing with joy. I had never had port before.

All that was swamped by the Great Depression of the thirties. It was far worse than what we are going through now because it could mean literal starvation. There was I, brought up to think that everyone must have an equal chance; I just couldn't cope with the injustice of what was going on all round me. Out of that my anger developed. Yet it never occurred to me to go into politics, even though Eleanor was a city councillor and an MP. I had been reared in the middle class. It was assumed that 'government' was done by the likes of us. We met directors of education and medical officers of health as social equals whereas politicians were a dirty lot. Local government was our opportunity to give public service, not to go into politics.

At that time, the social services were just developing so they looked to the voluntary societies for help. As paid workers, though we were called voluntary workers, woman ran school meals services, and holiday homes and youth clubs; childcare was pioneered in Liverpool by women. We were partners with the officials rather than with politicians. Politics was something to be kept out of.

Then in 1935 I got married – a great achievement in that generation of 'superfluous women'. My husband was a lecturer who later became Professor of Social Science at Liverpool University so it was out of the question that I should go on working. I had been a community worker but it never entered my head that I should go on, in spite of the fact that he was a passionate equality man. He had been trained at Oxford in the same moral philosophy as Eleanor.

Mercifully, fate intervened when the Second World War broke out and we were sent off to the West Indies where the Americans were having trouble with local people. It is sometimes said that where there's a riot, you'll find a Simey, but in this case the riot came first. The Americans had refused to share the swimming pools with local black people and this had provoked trouble.

So the government gathered together a team which included a farmer, an educationalist, my husband as a welfare expert and me as an (unpaid) community worker. They gave us a bag of gold and asked us to go out to the West Indies and 'keep the natives quiet'. We had no sooner arrived there than our hackles rose and I'm afraid we let it show. We had left Liverpool which had just had its biggest blitz and here we were, expected to wear long white gloves for dinner at Government House where there were always silver dishes of chocolates which you weren't allowed to touch till after the toast to the queen had been drunk. Smartly the Colonial Office descended on me and, with infinite tact, advised me that if my husband continued to make trouble, there would be no future for him in the Colonial Service. To which we both said, 'Thank God for that.'

My husband ended up – a Balliol philosopher, not a politician – with the governor of Jamaica threatening to put him in a concentration camp. All because he proposed a welfare system based on the assumption that everybody was equal. We gained much more than we gave to the West Indians. It was an education to meet the leaders of the independence movement; Eric Williams in Trinidad, Grantley Adams in Barbados and the great Norman Manley in Jamaica. When they talked about equality, with slavery so recent in their history, it really meant something. They were marvellous people, highly educated, but we were not supposed to visit their houses. Eventually a young ADC wangled a permit to get us off Jamaica and we managed to escape at dawn one day, only to be stranded in New York till we could get a ship home.

Our poor son had been dragged everywhere with us and educationally he was a wreck, so he went off to a progressive comprehensive who turned him into a splendid chap and totally convinced me that comprehensives are a good idea. We moved to Toxteth where we have been ever since and where we were the only 'university types' living in the area. The house had been a hostel for Chinese seamen and had been picked clean of every moveable fixture so we camped out like squatters for ages, and still do, for that matter.

Once we were home again, I headed straight for the Victoria Settlement, as a voluntary worker of course. But after the Beveridge Plan was accepted, I began to realise that the old voluntary tradition was breaking down. Was there any need for do-gooders in the welfare state? Or would I be more useful if I jumped the counter and became a politician?

What pushed me over the edge was an incident in the juvenile court. I had been a magistrate for years. A big white woman appeared before us with her two sons who were what we used to call half-castes, in schoolboy trouble. We sat behind a huge mahogany desk and she leaned across it with tears streaming down her face and begged us not to send the boys away. 'My husband is black and he has gone back to Ghana to make a home for us because there is no hope for lads like mine in Liverpool.' I was so ashamed that I went straight home and told my husband that I would have to go into politics to try to do something about the way we treated black people.

*

I became a city councillor in 1963. I was told by the police that Granby was the 'worst' ward in the country. Rachmanism,* poverty, unemployment, crime: you name it, we had it. What made it possible to go on was my immense respect for the people who lived there. In spite of all the burdens dumped on them, they never let up on the struggle to make decent lives for themselves, especially the women. Yet they were regarded as a burden, somehow substandard.

For all the difficulties and the frustration, I loved it. I had finally got a job that was bigger than me. I like to think that I was accepted as somebody who was there to give service. When my husband was bounced into being a life peer, I stuck to plain Mrs, but residents who asked me for a reference for a job would tell me to be sure to call myself a Lady because that would help them.

Because of what Eleanor called the 'peculiar constitution' of Liverpool, there have never been enough people here who are able and willing to speak out for those who are at the bottom of the heap. We have top dogs, who mostly live well away from the city and a huge mass of underdogs, unemployed, badly housed, unable to escape. I found myself pushed into trying to bridge the frightful gulf between them and us. The gulf between police and policed had disastrous results in 1981.

That was how we came to vote for Hatton. Nobody would speak for us or listen to us till up bobs this cocky young man. He was the only person who ever said 'Boo' to Maggie Thatcher on our behalf. No wonder we fell for him. To start with, all went well, and we really had hopes. Then rumours went round that his loyalty was not to us but to a mysterious body called Militant. It was a terrible betrayal. The only people who stood up to them were the locally born black community in Granby. They paid a stiff price. Bully boys beat them up. Grants for local projects were cut. I came in for a lot of stick myself. It was hard to persuade the outside world that

---

*Rachman was a slum landlord who used illegal methods to force tenants out of their homes.

what was going on could really happen in this country. In the end Kinnock came to our rescue but in spite of his brave confrontation, Militant still survives in Liverpool. And will do as long as we carry such a burden of deep deprivation.

People like Heseltine who mean so well always think they know what is good for us. They consult us ever so politely but keep a tight hold on the power to decide how much money shall be spent and what on. Garden festivals aren't much help to people who live in a poverty ghetto. I once had a fearsome argument with Heseltine over this. I don't think he can ever have been shouted at like that before – by an OAP from Toxteth, and a woman. He told me that there was no room in his scheme of things for types like me. Big business was the answer to Granby's problems.

My husband died in 1969. I was horrified when I woke the morning after his death and realised that I was a widow, and that I felt free. It was just what I felt when I crossed the Runcorn Bridge all those years ago and realised that now I could escape from school and be really me. He was a lovely man, but till then I had been the backroom girl, and content to be that. For the sake of my husband's career I had always played myself down and tried to be nice to the Vice Chancellor's wife and gone to the University Ladies Tea Club and done all the proper things. Then I woke that morning and it was all gone. I was free. I was taken aback by how I felt. I had been totally committed to the idea of family life but I had talents which were no use domestically, certainly no use to me as a university wife – in fact, they were a hindrance and made me feel resentful and frustrated.

I sometimes wonder if marriage as we talk of it is any longer viable. Real life isn't like that any more. We play games and wear white dresses at virgin weddings – at vast expense – but our actual lives are totally different. All our chatter about the royal family is just Cinderella stuff, completely out of touch with reality. Our welfare system is built on the supposition that we live in families. Mrs Thatcher once said there was no such thing as society. She would have been nearer the mark to ask if there was such a thing as a 'normal' family.

In fact, after more than twenty years as a 'free' female, I would go further. I think the whole women's movement has run into the sands. We have lost our sense of purpose. We started out by demanding equality so that we could take our share of the responsibility for what went on in the society we lived in. All we've won is the right to compete in a man's world, but we don't even do that on equal terms.

I'm not one for moment denigrating the tremendous progress we've made in the working world. It's been a long slog and knowing Alison Halford* has made me realise how far we still have to go. What bothers me is that in the process, we have had to learn to be men, and better men than men themselves are. Our experience as women is a handicap, not an asset. Try persuading the boss to upgrade you because you now have a child.

As a society we seem to have lost a whole dimension of life – the culture that says that there are social values, artistic and moral values, as well as material success. They are what we mean when we talk of 'feminine' values. Equality is all about getting women into top jobs but nothing is said about what they should give in return. Beveridge himself warned us that to opt for self-interest is to 'go down the primrose path to mutual destruction'. As a society we are destructing each other all right. I'm all for equal opportunities but not if they are only opportunities to better ourselves. What do we give as women to the society we live in? The answer is damn all.

It's up to the women's movement to give the lead in changing all this. Not because we are more compassionate than men – that would be nonsense – but because we know from our own experience there can be no question of turning our backs on people who need to be cared for. That's why so few of us make it to the top. But we also know that unless we create a society where our commitment to caring is valued we will never know real equality.

---

*Alison Halford was the highest-ranking British policewoman when she took her own police force, the Merseyside Constabulary, to an industrial tribunal, claiming that she was the victim of sex discrimination.

What is urgently called for is a new emancipation movement to set us all free – men and women – from outdated habits of mind from the past. It's not more crèches that are the answer but a change in attitudes, our own as well as everybody else's. There's a good Lancashire maxim that says, 'A man wrapped up in himself makes a very small parcel.' We need to set men free from the drudgery of a lifetime devoted to earning a living. And women must be freed from the impossible overload that is heaped on them so that we can all lead lives that are really worth living.

We've got ourselves a welfare state to make sure that we survive as individuals. The next step must be the creation of a welfare society, a truly caring community. That's the vision that could carry the women's movement forward into the unknown of the next century.

Jason Bell

CAROLINE MILLS

*'I want to live in
a society that is
genuinely a society'*

*Caroline Mills is a venture capitalist with a London bank and also a
Labour councillor on Camden Council. She is twenty-seven and has
lived in Camden all her life.*

My title at work is 'investment director', but if you are in the City
everyone is called a director and I don't think it is as grand as it
sounds. In my last job, I was called an 'assistant vice-president' and
my mother thought I must have been number three in the bank,
but there were about five thousand employees. In this business they
like to give you a name which implies that you run the show,
because you are always dealing with chief executives of companies
who don't want to feel they are dealing with a junior.

I always wanted to be a Labour councillor and I always wanted to
work in the private sector, although not necessarily in the City. My
father runs his own company and is also a Labour councillor and
my mother is a lawyer and they had a powerful influence on me.
There are lots of people I admire for sticking to their guns and
my father is one of them. He is on the moderate left but a sort of
pariah in the borough, where people either love him or hate him
for speaking out. I think he was a role model for me because he
certainly feels very strongly about having a leg in both the public
and private sector; he thinks I am immensely privileged to be
able to do that. I have always admired people who find their own

politics which isn't easy, especially if like me you are born into a liberal, left-of-centre family. Some of my earliest memories are of canvassing with my father and, as I grew older, it was natural for me to join the Labour Party and start establishing my own views. I represent an area in which I have lived all my life, I shop with the people I represent, I use all the council facilities and I went to the local comprehensive which I liked.

My job as a venture capitalist involves taking equity stakes in companies which we believe are going to succeed. Lots of people come to us, but nine out of ten aren't financeable for one reason or another. I have to make an assessment of the market (because we don't make money in dying markets), look for growth and very strong credible management, because they are the people we are backing.

It is a very competitive market and I tend to deal with the true blue end of Thatcherism: we back what we think are the winners; on the whole we are not in the business of backing start-ups. My long-term aim is to end up in business, but I thought working in the City would be a good way to get commercial experience. It is also interesting being involved with the Labour Party and working in the private sector, because many people in the private sector see the Labour Party as terrible bogeymen and there is still a widely held view in sections of the party that if you are making profits you must be whipping little children to dig in mines. I think I am in a position to take a fairly realistic view of both camps and, while it is absolutely crucial to have a left-of-centre government which is a prosperous government, it is the private sector which generates the prosperity for all the other things that we need to do. And I think sadly at the moment there isn't very much cross-fertilisation between the two.

My scepticism about Labour Party economic policy to date is that we were trying to present ourselves as a government capable of picking winners and history shows that the government isn't very successful at doing that – the commercial sector does it better. There is no liaison between the government and investors like us and I don't think it is proper that there should be. The private sector is trying to make money and if you are doing that, then you are not doing a government job. I think the Labour Party is more accepting of business than it was ten years ago. I feel more in tune with Labour Party politics than I did when I joined and it is very educational for somebody like me to go around companies and see the sorts of jobs that people do, because it is clear that the people who run this country never really see how most people live, what their schools are like or their homes or their jobs. I am sometimes appalled at the low wages people get and even more appalled to see managers make very small changes to what is really analogous work done by men and women, so the women are paid less.

The City is there to maximise profits and you have a government which allows them to do it to a degree which is detrimental to our manufacturing base. I don't think it is a question of telling the City they ought to be nicer; I think it is a government's responsibility to change things so that the whole economic policy isn't geared to lining the pockets of non-productive industries.

When I started getting interested in politics it was women's issues that affected me most and they are still issues about which I feel very strongly, but I think my real reason for being in the Labour Party is that I want to live in a society that is genuinely a society, and has a sense of looking after people who can't look after themselves. I feel that particularly strongly after having gone to a state school and seeing the insurmountable problems that other people have to overcome unless they are given help; the idea that they will just sort themselves out seems even more absurd if you have been to one of those schools, having come from a privileged background yourself. You see then that it only works in very few cases.

I do think I am quite a competitive person and maybe that is why I have got on working in a very male-dominated industry. I think feminism has failed to grab the imagination of many women, and indeed men, today. I am appalled by the number of working women who refuse to describe themselves as feminists and I think it is a generational problem because women of my mother's generation, who had a much greater sense of fighting for their right to work, certainly in their twenties, seemed much closer to the battle-front. I think young women today feel removed from it and want to get on with men. I don't think the way to change in business or the City is women's 'self-promotion' clubs, because all that is doing is replicating male networks and I think women have to behave in a different way and be committed to employing other women and working well with other women. There is a real obligation on women as they move up hierarchies to ensure they facilitate other women coming in and that if you are in a position to fight for child-care, you do that; you don't just say, 'Well I can afford a nanny', you go out and make a stand.

I would much prefer to have other women around and would always try to recruit another woman rather than a man because I do believe in positive discrimination, but if you look at the industry, the women leave by their mid-thirties because family life con-flicts with the hours. I work from 8.30 and don't get home until 7.30 or 8.00 and spend a couple of days a week outside London looking at different companies. I have a partner who votes Labour but is not a party member and obviously at some stage I would love to have children. I was brought up by nannies and, although I don't think that is ideal, I wouldn't have any guilt about doing the same thing myself. My mother was not the kind of person who could have stayed at home to be a cosy mum and be happy.

All the people that I work with, to a man, and they are nearly all men, are Tories. In my current job most of them don't know that I am a Labour councillor. Not because it is something I want to hide, but in my last job I got incredibly bored with people coming in and saying 'I would vote Labour but . . .' I felt no mission to convert them and I found it very frustrating. It is not a secret, but it is not something I advertise, partly because when I joined I was the only woman and the youngest by about ten years and I felt it was better to establish myself and then say: 'By the way, this is what I do' rather than have people think, if I left early, it was because I was going to a council meeting, whether or not I was. I usually have to go straight from work to council meetings. I am on Camden's

Policy and Resources and Social Services Committees. I don't think I would be that dedicated if I didn't like it, but I often find it the most enjoyable and interesting part of my day. I think serious politicians are very brave to continually stand up and say what they think and come off the fence all the time; it must be really tough to constantly have things thrown at you.

I joined the council when I was twenty-five and in some ways I think I was too young. I am not sure I had enough life experience to bring to it and you do spend all your evenings with people who are of a different generation, so I feel in some ways it is something I ought to have done later instead of spending my youth going to meetings! I constantly feel I can't do it properly; there are so many papers to read, so many meetings to attend, many of which I can't go to.

On the council I am very aware of the fact that what we do has a very real effect on people's lives. I think Camden Council has in the past been poorly run which is a shame because in the 1970s it was the sort of Labour council that people looked towards. Some of its problems can be blamed on central government – you can look across the country and see similar difficulties in other areas – but they were exacerbated by an over-politicised administration with imprudent financial planning and unrealistic expectations of Labour central government victories. Many of these chickens have now come home to roost.

A lot of the areas in which we have been forced to make cuts have been those that affect women most directly; we have cut playgroups and nursery provision in general. Nurseries, playgroups and libraries all come under the same budget, but because the middle classes are better at campaigning, libraries seem to be saved at the expense of playgroups which benefit women. Also the compulsory competitive tendering which has put contracts out to private tender has resulted in people, many of whom are women, being re-employed at lower wages.

It depresses me that the tea lady who works in my office believed she couldn't afford to vote Labour at the last election, which was down to a total failure to communicate on our part. I think the whole point of political parties is to communicate and persuade people, and if you have failed in doing that, you have failed completely. I think there were perhaps insurmountable obstacles to overcome but we still failed in what must be our primary objective.

PENELOPE LEACH

*'Children have
a right to have
their needs met'*

Penelope Leach is a Fellow of the British Psychological Society and author of the best-selling parents' guide Baby and Child. *She is an active campaigner for children's rights.*

I didn't set out to become involved with children and children's rights. When I was a student I never saw myself going into that area. I read history at Cambridge, but mostly I had fun. It's true that the psychology shelves became a draw from very early on, but I didn't change subjects. When I'd done my degree I wished I had, because by that time I knew I wanted to work in child development, but I was the wrong side of an arts-science barrier and had to work my way sideways into psychology by starting off with a social work diploma. There were still reasonable student grants then or I couldn't have done it.

I was always politically involved. My stepfather, Michael Ayrton, was the grandson of a suffragette – Hertha Ayrton's house was a refuge for women released from prison in the cat-and-mouse days – and his mother, Barbara Ayrton-Gould, was the first woman chair of the Labour Party. From around fourteen I was brought up in a household where those values were taken for granted. I was around the New Left Review, CND, the Committee of a Hundred, Prisoners of Conscience. I never thought about sex discrimination in my youth because it simply did not exist at home. I also went to an all-girls grammar school so I didn't have to find out for myself in adolescence. It may sound privileged; it *was* privileged. I was never formally part of the women's movement. For anyone involved in issues around childbirth and child-rearing it was very difficult to find a place in it because, for many years, biologically female concerns were often seen as anti-feminist. Later on when I published a Penguin Special *Who Cares? A New Deal for Mothers and their Young Children*, I got a lot of stick. The book was published just as Margaret Thatcher came to power and although I never saw it as having a Tory message – far from it – that was how it was seen by some people.

While I did my social work diploma immediately after graduating, I worked in local authority children's departments and then did a year's research at the Home Office on juvenile crime. That earned my way into LSE's graduate psychology department and research into the differential effects on children of different kinds of upbringing. Later on, with a Medical Research Council fellowship, I turned that around and studied twins to show that even if you have two babies of the same sex, at the same time, their individual differences inevitably mean that you treat them differently. Parents affect babies but babies affect them just as much. Sounds obvious now, but that was the early sixties: the 'blank slate' approach to infants was only just ending.

By this time I was doing research and teaching psychology at LSE and it began to occur to me that the people who could really use the mass of new findings about child development that were being passed around in academic papers were parents – and they had no access to it. It was up to 'mother dear' to *do* her best, but up to the doctor to *know* best. There was a real chasm between parents and professionals. When our daughter, Melissa, was born I felt as if I'd got one foot either side of that chasm. My first book, *Babyhood: infant development from birth to two years*, was a deliberate try at bridging it. The chasm's not so deep now but it's still there. I've always loathed rigid divisions of status and roles that patronise and limit people.

*

Then and now, I took aspirations to a redistribution of wealth and increasing social equity for granted. I still find it surprising that other people don't. Maybe that makes me naive but I was truly astonished at how few people were outraged when the Chancellor cut the top rate of income tax from 50 per cent to 40 per cent. I can't see how people can feel that a few per cent of tax is worth holding on to in a society where basic values are being eroded for everybody. Society is developing in such a way that people's status, their self-image, is totally tied to the work they do for money and the amount they earn. If you can't buy and sell it, it isn't worth having – and if you can, it is, however sleazy it may be. I really do not believe that the profit motive is enough for people. Of course I'm not quarrelling with women's right to equal opportunities or with the economy's need for women in the workplace. But if women are to have truly equal opportunities in the world that was traditionally men's, men also have to be equally involved in the world that was traditionally women's, otherwise how does anyone propose that children should be reared, or any non-commercial functions carried out, come to that? At the moment there is a truly terrifying lack of respect for children; for their changing needs and for the people – parents – who try to meet them. A lot of children feel that they're in the way. What else can they feel when they wear keys round their necks to let themselves into empty houses two hours ahead of anyone else – and when their 'holidays' mean boredom and loneliness?

Of course the answer's not a return to 'women at home'. The home-based productive female network within which children used to start life is long gone in most of the UK and has been since the Second World War (though it suited fifties' politicians, who needed to clear jobs for returning soldiers, to pretend otherwise). Maybe it's a pity. Maybe children got a better apprenticeship to adult life when they *were* part of busy households where women were doing lots of important things apart from looking after them. But history never runs backwards. Women who *do* stay at home with children now – whether because they can't get jobs or daycare places or because they feel it's best for the children – often find themselves alone all day with a single toddler in a small flat on the tenth floor of an estate that's virtually empty because almost everybody else is at work . . . That's no way of life for either of them. No wonder the workplace looks like Nirvana. No wonder partnerships break down. If there are no other close adults in your life, your sexual partner has to stand in for father, mother, confidante, girlfriend . . . Nobody can, or ought to have to be, everything to anybody.

I think real answers have to come out of fundamental changes of attitudes; sharing responsibility for children equally between parents – and having that acknowledged in the workplace from managing director to apprentice; making the communities where people live and the things they do for love, as central to their lives as the places where they work and the things they do for money. I can't tell you the number of times I have been told by women expecting their first babies that they have just met their neighbours and made friends with them after five years.

It's sad that we make such hard work out of our children. I thought we were doing that in the 1970s. I wrote *Baby and Child* because there was so much guilt among parents (let's face it, among mothers!) about babies being too fat, or being 'late' in walking or talking or, heaven help us, sitting on pots. I thought it would help to think a bit more about children as people, rather than performers; to have a bit more fun and less duty bringing them up. We're making even harder work of it now, though. That's really what the edition I wrote for the nineties had to say. It's truly difficult to find time and space for a child – and stay solvent.

Putting children in daycare is the obvious – and at the moment the fashionable – answer. I'm battling against the kind of entrepreneurial group care for babies and pre-nursery children which is spreading here from the United States. A lot of parents prefer day-nurseries to child-minders or other parent-substitutes. They're easier to police; they're a business so they're more reliable (they don't get pregnant or take holidays); they don't involve parents in such personal relationships (one mother told me, disgustedly, 'You have to make friends with your child-minder and *crawl* if you're late to pick your child up; all the nursery wants is "good-morning" and my cheque') and they are seen as being in the honourable tradition of pre-school education. The argument is that if nursery school is a good preparation for school, day-nursery must be a good preparation for nursery school. That's a fallacy. Nursery schooling is essential because by two and a half or three years, children need some time with other children and with teachers. But babies and toddlers who can't even speak or wipe their own bottoms yet do not benefit from either. They do most of their learning by being one-to-one with an adult – parent or other – who thinks they are gorgeous and will help them think so too. American-style daycare centres are already here and more are planned. They take babies all day from as young as six weeks and parents are putting down names the moment pregnancy is confirmed. New Etons? Well they're certainly not affordable by anyone on an average wage or by any lone parent. I find the whole idea of infant care in a competitive profit-market totally abhorrent. There'll inevitably be pressure on adult–infant ratios: one adult to three babies may sound fine, and one to four or five is regarded as OK, but do you know any mothers of triplets? And how about raising the profit margin by giving toddlers smaller pieces of paper to draw on?

We're in a new kind of society having old-style children and I think we need to look for different ways of integrating the two. The group-care model isn't right for under-twos; a state grant for women to stay at home isn't right for women. Maybe we need parenting sabbaticals within the framework of the work-world, and parent-run, community-based family centres as a modern version of traditional and extended-family networks . . .

Children's needs are not being met in the UK – and nobody knows that better than parents. And children do have a *right* to have their needs met, just like anybody else. It isn't enough to see them as 'objects of concern'. The phrase 'children's rights' has crept into our language since the United Nations Convention on the Rights of the Child but it hasn't had much effect on our actions. We don't even respect children's basic *human* rights. We argue about who should be allowed to hit children, and how hard, for example. But why on earth is it acceptable for anyone to hit them at all? All adults take legal protection from inter-personal violence for granted. The Children's Rights Unit – and a plan for a children's commissioner – have been started because we think there should be constant monitoring of the effect on children of all social policy. At the moment, there's almost none. In all the talk about the forty-eight hour week, for example, I've seen not one mention of the importance to children of there being at least one day in the week when parents cannot be expected to go to work. The new Children Act has gone a long way, but it cannot do what it ought to do because there just aren't the resources to practise what it preaches. Do you know there are local authorities who have closed their lists to new, vitally needed child-minders because they haven't the resources to carry out the registration procedure?

My despair is that if we had got a change of government in 1992, there might just have been time to turn things around, but since we didn't, there probably won't be. I think we're seeing a catastrophic deterioration in the value we put on children; on the people who care for them – and other necessarily dependent people; indeed on people in general. We are living to work instead of of working to live and, as unemployment rises, more and more people are left with nothing: no money, nothing to do that feels meaningful, no pride. And it's not all due to world recession either. We are going back to a selective education system, a two-tier health service, we're maybe even going to have workfare. How can we say to children, 'There are equal opportunities for everyone; there are rewards for effort; it's worth working hard' when they can see it's a con because you're no more likely to get a job or a decent place to live if you've got A levels than if you leave school at sixteen.

It frightens me that we're prepared to have children in bed and breakfast accommodation when everybody knows that's unacceptable on grounds of health and development. It frightens me that we are breeding children who can see no sensible reason for behaving decently to one another; who vandalize public property because they don't feel it belongs to them and who have little respect for the law because the society it represents gives them no social justice. It frightens me most of all that we have let a society evolve in which just having a child is a major socio-economic disadvantage. I think we really do risk some kind of social breakdown and that it will start with our children as they become betrayed and disaffected adolescents, and then young adults who see that everything needs to be changed and feel helpless to change anything. Yes, I blame the government. There is so much that it could do but it does so little and adds insult to injury by making a virtue of not intervening; of leaving everything to market forces and free enterprise. Individuals and groups are doing all they can but can only go so far without political backing.

NAJMA HAFEEZ

'A struggle to be taken seriously'

Najma Hafeez was born in Pakistan and came to Britain with her family in the early 1960s. She is now a Labour councillor, the only Asian woman on Birmingham City Council, and hopes to become a Labour MP.

I was born in Pakistan and came to England with my family in 1964 for economic and educational reasons. We were originally from India, but after the partition we had nothing left over there and we were being persecuted against as Moslems, so we moved to Pakistan and then here. When we came to Birmingham, we moved in with my uncle's family in Station Road in King's Heath – the only Asian family in a predominantly white area. There was only the attic for us to live in, which was very large, and I can remember having to haul coal in a push-chair and the feel of the lino, cold on the feet. My mother was very much affected by the weather and developed asthma straight away so she was constantly ill. I was the second oldest but my elder brother hadn't arrived from Pakistan because of complications with the immigration laws. He was parted from us for two years and that had a very significant effect on him and us. We have never really gelled together and he has remained distant and insecure from the rest of us. It also devastated my mother.

In those early years, Mum was very ill so I had my younger brother and sister to look after. We were materially quite deprived and poor and I remember thinking it was not fair. My father worked in a factory but it was very racist and we weren't able to buy a house because he couldn't get a mortgage. It was a very hard struggle for us all, especially my parents.

When I went to my primary school, I remember everyone gawping at me. My first language was Punjabi and Urdu and my dad had trained us to say our name and address and date of birth in English, which at first was all I knew, although I picked more up very quickly. I was the odd one out in the school so it was a period I didn't like very much. I remember at my secondary school, my teacher asked me my name in a sort of sign language because she didn't expect me to speak English and I just said: 'My name is Najma Hafeez and why are you pulling faces at me?' The rest of the kids thought it was hilarious and that broke a barrier.

There was a lot of discrimination and prejudice. Children would be quite cruel. Geography lessons were all about the third world and I resent that phrase to this day. It is so patronising, implying that we are not first or second, so I always used to feel ashamed and uncomfortable and not nice. I remember another Jewish girl, who wasn't in my year, became my friend because we were the odd ones out. Eventually I got over all that, mixed in and made friends with white kids.

At home we had very strong cultural ties. We had some Gujerati people living close to us who were very traditional Moslems, like the Orthodox Jews. We had to learn the Holy Koran with them, because there were not very many mosques around then, and this was sometimes difficult because their language was so different that we couldn't understand them. We were also taught by a relative who came from Pakistan and who happened to be a Mullah. We wore the traditional clothes and on my first day at secondary school, where the uniform was bottle green, my mother sent me along in a shiny royal blue dress with white satin trousers, which she had made especially for me, and great bigs bows in my hair. She meant well, wanting me to look smart, but I remember going into the assembly and sitting there like a pumpkin because everybody was in spanking new bottle green uniforms and I just felt totally ridiculous and went home to tell my mum she had got it wrong. But she was brilliant and got me bottle green cloth and made me a special new uniform. I think I must have been a confident kid, otherwise it would have affected me more.

As I said, we lived in King's Heath where the houses were nice and we adopted an elderly white couple nearby as 'granny and grandad'. My mum and dad really made an effort with the neighbours. We had Asian friends in Sparkbrook, but that made an impression on me because it was so different and run-down and I thought that, and the immigration system, were really unfair. I was aware of families being parted and people not getting into the country and as I got older there was no alternative to the Labour Party. I couldn't imagine anyone in the Conservative Party ever helping us.

My father was a staunch Labour supporter and he was very much affected by the discrimination around him in the factory. He had one or two good friends in senior positions and they would come to our house and my dad would call them 'Sir' and I would be shocked because I had never seen my father in such a deferential position. This really did annoy me because I didn't like him being so subservient. I wanted everyone to be equal. When I asked him why he did it, he would always tell me I wouldn't understand yet. It was only later that I discovered that, while many people treated my family in a racist way, these men had used their names to help get my dad a loan from the bank, which started him off in his original business. Growing up in that climate, it was impossible not to loathe the system and want to do something about it.

I was absent from school quite a lot, because I had to look after my brothers and sister, but as soon as I reached puberty pressure from the community developed and I left school at sixteen and was married at eighteen. Although my own arranged marriage failed, there are very many excellent examples of stable and happy arranged marriages all around us. I feel mine only failed because of the horrendous conflict between my own personal aspirations as a young Asian woman, wanting higher education and a career, and my husband's at the time. After my divorce, I finally got to do my degree and I was determined to have a career of my own. I also got involved in the Labour Party after opening the door to a man from the party and thinking: 'Who does he think he is and what does he know about us and equal rights?' I got really uptight with him and he suggested I went to a meeting at the local branch, so I went and saw all these teachers and social workers and other middle-class professionals pontificating and thought: 'What do they know about us?' The anger was there so I got sucked in, got involved with writing the newsletter and becoming the constituency secretary.

It was through the Labour Party that I met Albert, who was local MP Tom Litterick's agent at the time. We got married in 1983 and are both now on the council. He of course had to convert to Islam. I feel that discrimination and prejudice were still there but I was able to ignore it, although I don't think many other women are, which makes me very angry because they shouldn't have to get used to it. My family were increasingly concerned about my political involvement, because any possibility of me marrying a nice Asian boy was getting more and more remote. They had great difficulty accepting my marriage to Albert. I now have two sons, and although I am quite westernised, I want to bring my boys up the way I have been brought up, because it was very secure and stable. There are many positive things about my culture and religion. It is a great shame that Islam has been misrepresented by many people for their own personal reasons, which have nothing to do with the pure religions and way of life. I want my boys to understand other religions, but they need one stable creed, so my oldest boy is learning the Koran, and so will the younger one. I think they feel closer to me culturally and religiously because my family is around all the time, and is a great support as well as an inspiration.

The first council seat I fought was Selly Oak on Birmingham City Council. Nobody stopped me because it was not a winnable seat and I thought it would be good experience. Then I was asked to stand for Fox Hollies, the ward which I now represent. There was massive opposition to me standing here because it was a safe white area and people thought I would lose the seat and that would be very negative for the Labour Party. They thought I should stand for an Asian area, but I didn't see why I should. I feel it is very important to prove to people that an Asian woman can represent anyone, anywhere. I won the seat and people were surprised, some were even angry, but I am still here and I have been reselected ever since unanimously.

I feel conscious that sometimes I come across as bitter, which I suppose I am because it has been a struggle to be taken seriously, and as an Asian woman, you face discrimination on two fronts. The white community is resistant because I am different and on the other hand the Asian community is very very uncomfortable with me because I voice my opinions and have done things of which they don't approve, like marrying Albert, and they are frightened that their daughters might want to emulate me.

About five years ago fundamentalism became an issue. Moslem families feel increasingly threatened by western culture. This led to girls and young women running away from home: one of the biggest problems in the Asian community at the moment is the issue of girls wanting to move away from home and assert themselves, so the families react by wanting to ignore women like me or closet their daughters or send them to Pakistan as soon as possible if they get out of line. Many families have become very strict, which has only compounded the problem. Since I became chair of Birmingham's Social Services Committee, I have set up helplines for Asian girls and women who have run away from home and these are extremely important and successful. I have also set up a helpline for families because I feel they need our support and to know that their girls are safe. We have also got hostels for women and girls so they don't have to go on the streets and get picked up by sharks who want to take them out of the country. I believe the situation is worsening for Asian women; the families are closing in and young girls are being monitored from a much younger age than I was, and pressures on Asian girls are greater. There is more opportunity, enlightenment and temptation for them on one hand, but more clawing back on the other. That is why it is critical for us to create support networks which bridge this gap between the conflict of young people and their families. I think most families in all communities face generational conflicts but in Britain today this is a greater cultural problem to the Asian communities. Boys and young men are just as vulnerable as girls, and they need help too.

In response to this problem, there have been many private religious schools set up and I am concerned at the numbers of private, single-sex Moslem schools now being established without adequate provision or standards. There are, of course, many excellent ones, but I still fear those that do not meet the necessary educational standards and those which are not even registered with any legitimate body.

As I see it, there is as much discrimination against women in the Labour Party and for an Asian woman it is even worse. There are seventeen Asian councillors out of 164 on Birmingham City Council and I am the only Asian woman. It is a very lonely position and I would very much like it to change; for many more Asian women to come forward and help to struggle against some of the inequality we face. I am prepared to go further away to get selected for a parliamentary seat, but I would like a seat where I am selected for the qualities and representation I can give to men and women, not simply because I am an Asian woman. When I stood for selection for the parliamentary seat of Birmingham Small Heath, I faced considerable personal and family abuse which in one way made me more determined, but in another way confirmed to me that women do have to fight harder than men. I am still hoping that one day I will get a seat and be able to fulfil my ambition to serve the community. Sometimes I am very frustrated about the lack of support for women, particularly mothers, but that usually confirms my commitment to doing something about it. The only way seems to be to obtain some power in order to improve and change the present system.

As a working woman and a working mother, I have to be quite ruthless with my time and sometimes be willing to compromise, which I do. I just hope when my boys, Omar and Firaz, get older, they will be proud of me and say that at least their mum did something to try and change the system for the better.

HELENA
KENNEDY

*'We have to take the
law by the throat'*

*Helena Kennedy is a QC and an active campaigner for women's
rights, both within the legal profession and outside. Three years ago she
joined forces with other progressive barristers to set up the Doughty
Street Chambers.*

I've always said that when I'm old I'll write my autobiography and
call it *Never the Gangster – always the Moll*. Like most women, I
was given the softer case work – like family work – when I started
out, so I have a lot of experience of representing women. I don't
feel any sense of loss about that because my involvement with
civil liberties campaigns has meant that I've also done other very
interesting, demanding cases, like the Irish cases. But there still
aren't many women around doing very heavy criminal cases. There
remains a feeling that adversarial advocacy is not appropriate for
women, that it is not nice to see them fighting a case hard, that it is
not very ladylike.

The intake to Law School now includes about 46 per cent
women, but we are not seeing very many working-class women
coming in. There are still shocking areas of discrimination, they
are just hidden and less explicit now. We have moved away from
the era when chambers said they wouldn't have women at all,
which was the case when I first came to the Bar. That has gone
partly because it has become unlawful to say it, but also because it

does not make for good public relations, nor is it good for business, so there are very few chambers around now that don't have at least some women. But even though the 'no-female' policy has been dispensed with, you see women more visibly at the bottom end of chambers and the line is often taken that, as the last two people taken on were females, even if the next best candidate is female we don't need to take her on. So there isn't real equality yet.

One of the axes I have to grind is that sexist policies hide behind the notion of merit. When John Major put together his first cabinet there was a sigh of relief that Maggie had gone – they were relieved to have no women, they wanted to be chaps together again. But even the Tory papers were asking where the women in the cabinet were and his answer was that the cabinet was appointed on merit and when there is enough 'merit' the women will get in. But merit is not an objective test – it is a subjective test defined by men and, in chambers where women are taken on, they have to conform to a very strict male notion of what is good. There is still much under-valuing of women and of what women can and do bring to any profession or job.

The savage reduction in grants has made it harder for anyone from a less affluent background to get in, and there is tough competition for scholarships. Individual sets of chambers are supposed to give scholarships to assist pupils through their lean years, but we are finding that more investment is committed to men than to women. The figures show that something happens between the women coming through and doing well in exams, and women getting scholarships and places in chambers, which they don't do in commensurate numbers. Then there is the hurdle of trying to combine a career with a family life. Many women have to pay rent for their space when they aren't there, even though other people might be sitting at their desks and using their facilities. Once you have had a family, the idea of trying to get back in can be difficult. That is something we are trying to deal with by campaigning for full-scale maternity leave and ensuring that women shouldn't have to pay any levy while they are out.

I had been campaigning for these things over the years and was fobbed off fairly regularly, so I eventually decided that the only way to get change was to actually stand for election, which I did. A large proportion of the Bar Council is not elected, they get there by being representatives of circuits, and there are people there who aren't representatives of anything at all. But there is a section that is electable, so I stood and got elected and the first thing I did was to pick up the issue of opportunities for women, their appointment as judges and so on.

Eventually a sex discrimination committee was established and it is working, partly because we've got good people on it who really are putting their time in, and partly because we commissioned a serious study of what happens to women's careers, so we now have the material to prove our case.

I have three children and have been very lucky to have two wonderful nannies in succession, which was the only solution for me because of the hours. When I had Keir, who is now nine, I got a place in a nursery, but I found it didn't work because I couldn't get there to collect at 5.30 so I had to have someone who came in. Lots of young women who campaign for a crèche at the Bar realise as soon as they start trying to juggle that a nursery doesn't work very practically because, especially with a criminal practice, you are often at different courts in different areas which leads to problems when you have to go back and pick up your child.

I don't feel that I have missed out on time with my children. With each successive baby, I took more time off because I felt more confident that my practice wasn't going to disappear and that there was a place in the world for me when I went back. I find ways of making time to be with the children. For a long time I think career women indulged in macho mothering and felt that to say that there was a problem would somehow count against them. Your children were supposed to be invisible. I looked at these women, who were proud of the fact that they were giving birth and back at work two days later, and knew I didn't want that. It seemed crazy and infinitely preferable to admit that it wasn't always easy, that it was bloody hard, that there are no Superwomen and that the juggling takes its toll on you and that's why you've got bags under your eyes and dust on the skirting board. You've got to tell everybody the truth. It will continue to be like that while the world of work does not take account of family life for both men and women.

I started feeling uncomfortable, as I became more successful, with newspaper articles which gave the impression that somehow there were thirty hours in my day and that I was Superwoman. I thought it much more important for people to see that very often the juggling act gets out of control. There are times when you feel things are working very well and there are other times when you feel that your work is completely swallowing up your life, and other times when you think: 'I should have got that case' and you want to be out there doing it. Getting it right is never easy.

I have no ambitions to become a judge, but I am ambitious as a courtroom performer. I'm an advocate, not a lawyer's lawyer. I wouldn't be interested in being a judge in the circuit court and to be a judge in the High Court demands that you are a particular kind of lawyer who finds points of law interesting. I am not that cerebral, I'm astute and streetwise and I still like taking sides, so I can't see myself readily in the judicial role (although I might feel differently about that in ten years' time). I am, however, interested in the policy of law. I would like to be involved in judicial training for example, and I think we should be setting up a judicial college where judges are actually discussing issues with real people in the community and other professions. It happens in other countries, but here it is less thorough-going.

There are still problems of discrimination against women in our courts. It's partly due to the attitudes of judges. However, sometimes the law itself fails women. We see this in the definition of the provocation law and whether it works as a defence for women whom we know don't usually respond in the face of violence, partly because of conditioning and partly because of physical disadvantage. However, they do sometimes respond to prolonged psychological and physical abuse, but the law has developed to reflect a male view of the world, requiring sudden loss of control rather than the slow burn response of women.

Then there is the business of the sexual double standards in the prostitution law, in which the prostitute is responsible for all the venality and not the consumer. Even though they have technically introduced the idea of kerb-crawling as an offence, it is rarely used because nobody takes men using prostitutes particularly seriously.

I also see a case for changing the rape laws. When I go to talk to women's groups there's a genuine feeling that to be buggered or to have an implement enter into your vagina is just as horrifying as penis penetration. It is a very male view of the world which dictates that somebody else's penis penetrating a woman is an awful crime when in fact for women, it is all about invasion of their being. The penalty for using a broom handle in somebody's vagina is not deemed to be the same as penile violation because of the risk of venereal disease or AIDS, but a lot of women would like rape to be defined to take account of other kinds of penetration. Why can't we have a gender-free definition of rape? There is a sort of mythology in the court, which is partly to do with bad women and partly to do with men being like steam engines who can't stop once they've got a head of steam up. So it is deemed unfair for women to expect them to accept 'no' and if a woman has consented to kissing, she is actually deemed to be asking for it. That is unacceptable.

Judicial training would make a huge difference. If all lawyers were informed on issues like rape and sexuality and were conscious about changing attitudes and had to apply them in the courtroom, it would make a real change to the way in which lawyering was done and eventually to the kind of judges we got. They do it in the United States but there is a sort of arrogance here which arises out of the male clubiness, which we have got to dispel. I'm not a barbarian, or one of those who would tear down the Inns of Court, which are very beautiful, and terrific for those who want weddings or functions and the occasional dinner there. But the idea that you have the Inns of Court running the profession which in turn is run by benchers – judges, or potential judges – is really quite appalling. We are supposed to be an independent profession, independent of the judges before whom we argue and fight our cases, yet that is where the cloning of the next generation of judges takes place. They become the image of the ones that have gone before. People come from Singapore and other parts of the world to the Inns of Court to 'eat their dinners'.* The idea is that you are imbuing young lawyers with the ethos of the Bar in the process, but they are also being drawn into a club, creating conformity and making sure they don't break rank and rock the boat. It is an atmosphere that can never be conducive to women, but of course most men get to like it.

I ate my dinners when I had to, although becoming a lawyer wasn't really a great life plan. I wanted to study in London – one of my sisters was living here and I came down for a summer holiday job and liked it. My family were very upset with the idea of me not being in Glasgow, where I was brought up. My father was a despatch hand on the *Daily Record*. He was an unskilled worker, a thoughtful man who valued education but never had the chance himself. Both my parents left school at fourteen and were political. My father was a strong trade unionist.

Most people feel the law has nothing to do with their lives. They do not see it as a useful tool or a method for obtaining redress. It is a view with which I still sympathise. My own parents would never set foot in a lawyer's office for fear of the cost and because they felt it was not for the likes of them. The result is that many ordinary people forfeit their rights. The new legal aid cuts will exacerbate the problem. Lawyers who believe in social justice have to put themselves at the service of those who have no voice within the system and we have to de-mystify the law. Unfortunately, too many lawyers who start out committed are seduced by the legal culture. But I still feel like an outsider, which I think is an advantage.

We set up the Doughty Street Chambers because we thought it would be good to have a group of lawyers involved with civil liberties cases and human rights issues, who shared a kind of understanding about the purpose of the law in terms of the public

---

*Law students who intend to read for the Bar have to eat a certain number of dinners at the Inns of Court to which they are attached.

interest. It is very nice to work with people that you get on with so well. We all do very different work and a lot of us do other things away from court like writing, lecturing and broadcasting which might improve us as lawyers, rather like doing research makes better teachers; it is the difference between a stagnant pool and a babbling brook. We are working hard to increase the number of women and we have put in place a policy on maternity leave. There is a strong intellectual bent here, which is challenging, and we want to try to change the law and move it on, in the way that some American and Australian lawyers are more prepared to do. British lawyers tend not to be as creative; we need to be saying: 'The law is not working here. How can we make it work? How can we get more out of it?'

I receive opinions from people who say that their lawyers have told them that they haven't got a case, or that they can't appeal. If you look at the opinion, it often says something like: 'Yours is the worst miscarriage of justice I've ever seen, but I can't advise you to appeal because there are no grounds.' We mustn't accept that. We have to take the law by the throat.

When I took silk [became a QC] two years ago, I was asked whether I had now joined the establishment and the answer is that an awful lot of the issues that had me labelled as a radical lawyer were issues on which the establishment has now had to bite the bullet. There were problems in the Irish cases, the issue of race was being denied and is now showing up in statistics, there were problems with the way women were treated by the courts. These days, you don't have to go very far to find people who would agree that those issues are mainstream and have to be addressed. Of course the establishment is still trying to hang on to its rituals, like the dinners and the wigs, which make them different, but eventually I believe even the wig will go. I am in favour of keeping the gown, because in America, where they don't wear one, there is the problem of clients commenting on their lawyer's clothes or appearances. I'm told that women lawyers then start taking advice about colour to match a certain type of case, whether it is emotional or not, whether you are opening your case to the jury and so on. So

I think there is a point in a sort of uniform so you are identified as the people who are doing the lawyering.

But forget about the wigs. If necessary, they can remain for ceremonial occasions, but the courts should feel as though they belong to all the people, that they belong to the present, not some bygone era. I was once accused by Lord Denning of wanting to turn them into American courtrooms where people smoked and told each other jokes. That was absurd. You can have a degree of formality without it having to be other-worldly and Alice in Wonderlandish and that change in the legal culture is what we need.

FRANCES PARTRIDGE

'I have never liked conventions'

Frances Partridge, born in Bloomsbury in 1900, is a writer and a lifelong pacifist. After Cambridge she became close to the Bloomsbury set and married Ralph Partridge, also a writer. Her books include several volumes of her memoirs and diaries.

My mother was an intelligent and enlightened woman, the child of an archdeacon in New Zealand. She was married in a time when women were expected simply to look after their husbands and families, but like her, I have always valued the company of people who think for themselves. She was more political than my father and an early feminist – a suffragist rather than a suffragette because she hated violence. Several suffragists of that time, like Mrs Fawcett, came to stay with us when I was a little girl, and I walked in a procession carrying a flag saying 'Votes for Women' when I was nine. After my father's death, my mother became an ardent Labour supporter and joined the party. In the early part of the century many middle-class women took part in less directly political activities helpful to the poor, like attending care committees, as she did. It seems to me looking back that it was a much nicer world then than now.

I remember being very impressed by some of the speeches I heard when I was about nine or ten. I particularly remember Mrs Sidgwick [a prominent suffragist] as a very delightful and rational person. I have always been very much in favour of rationalism. I don't mean that I don't value emotions, I do; but I feel they should be guided by rationalism. Maybe I was a feminist in that I wanted an end to discrimination against women, but I can also remember thinking that being a man had certain drawbacks. Today I think I feel there is more urgency to deal with poverty and issues like shutting down hospitals.

I got to know the Bloomsburys when I came down from Cambridge and, greatly as I admired and loved them, I confess still to being surprised by the effect they have had on subsequent generations. Rationality and integrity were very important to them and we all had very strong feelings about standing by our beliefs – although we weren't solemn at all and had a lot of fun. I lost my belief in religion when I was about eleven and I have never come back to it, but it seems to me that money is God now and that is an appalling thing and also it is what this awful selling of arms is about. Now people seem to be competing for greater and greater wealth all the time and showing off how rich they are. I have always disliked that along with the class system. As for the royal family, I am sorry for them because I think they have a beastly job, but I wouldn't mind at all if we didn't have them.

Virginia Woolf was a literary genius who also thought politically; her book *Three Guineas* had a lot of sound sense as well as feminism in it, and is as true now as it was then although I don't think it was appreciated as much as it deserved. I suppose my friends and I were unconventional. I have never liked conventions – because by definition they are imposed, not thought out, and I believe that all values should be decided upon freely by people for themselves. My pacifism is my most deeply held belief and I feel about it as many people feel about religion, which I haven't got. My diary, *A Pacifist's War*, describes our life during the Second World War. Of course I was passionately interested in the war (who could not be?) but at the time I never meant to publish it. When I did, the publisher wanted me to put in everything disagreeable that anyone had said to us but there wasn't an awful lot of hostility towards us because of our views.

My husband Ralph had fought very bravely in the First World War and won a number of decorations, but by the end he had realised all too clearly what war meant. Eighteen years later, we went to France to see the battlefields – an extraordinary and daunting experience. I can see now in a flash those miles of crosses in the graveyards; and even after eighteen years the ploughs were still turning up bones. It brought it all harrowingly back to Ralph that in those places dozens of men had fought and died. By the Second War he was too old to fight, so they called him up for non-combatant work and after much consideration he decided to go and testify to his beliefs at the tribunal, giving his reasons for not taking part.

The Second World War was much less of a muddle politically. Hitler was a monster; he was also the result of the First War, since each war breeds another. The Danes didn't fight and were respected, and although people say we have had thirty years of peace now, it seems to me we have had nothing but war somewhere in the world. Just because it is someone else's war it doesn't mean we can ignore it. After such fearful destruction, we are left with bitterness and the same problems we started with. I take a terribly gloomy view of the future now after all those years of frustrated ideals and it seems to me that, apart from a very few politicians, people with ideals and beliefs have gone out of politics. I am horrified by the nuclear pile-up and the fact that we have helped arm people like Saddam Hussein, because while there are weapons there will be wars, and if you put a weapon into the hands of a crazy man you will get shot. I don't think there is much of a pacifist movement now, but I do think that if there were more women in charge, there would be fewer calls to arms. I think the mere fact of being the mother of children makes a difference. Women are born with an instinct to preserve life rather than destroy it.

I suppose it is true to say that arts and literature came before politics for the Bloomsbury set, but we had amongst us remarkably brilliant people who took part in politics like Maynard Keynes. He wasn't totally pacifist but he was supportive of us who were and he believed in people upholding their beliefs. I notice that people often bristle when you use a word like 'egalitarianism', about which I feel very strongly. They either feel there is no such thing or that it is a very bad thing to strive for. In my view equality of opportunity is one of the most important things there is.

I have quite a lot of young friends, because I have lost so many old ones, and I think they are, in some ways, more open and approachable than we were, which is good. They are much more et ease with their seniors; even my great-grandchildren call me by my christian name. But they seem to treat their lives in a temporary way. They embark on relationships and marriages not expecting them to last. I believe marriage is a serious and rewarding relationship, to be worked at, and I never had any moments when I thought mine wouldn't last. Ralph and I had a very good and warm marriage, the secret of which was communication. I credit Ralph with that because, although he was a very masculine man, he had certain feminine qualities. He was very interested in people and psychology, he was sympathetic and always wanted to get to the truth. I never knew that you could talk so intimately to someone else until I met him. He was always a tremendous support. We loved discussing things and people who used to come and stay at our house, Ham Spray, used to say they heard us talking together from the moment we went to the bathroom in the morning together. It was a very equal relationship. I have long since stopped treating men and women differently. Even after thirty years, I still miss Ralph terribly.

My last volume of memoirs described my attempt to make a life after Ralph died. I never had publication of my diaries in mind when I wrote them. After Ralph's death my diary became someone to talk to. Also there have been events, which at times seem to dominate my life. The next volume includes the death of my son in December 1963 of a heart attack, leaving a young wife and a two-month-old baby who is now the mother of my great-grandchildren. I went through a very bad time when my husband and son died and loneliness and sadness get worse with age. I forget my age until someone in a bus or train is kind and helpful and then I feel rather ashamed of myself because I am very anxious to be as independent as I can.

I am ninety-two and it is rather a dismal age to be with nothing much to look forward to, although I would love to see the Labour Party come in as I hoped it would at the last election. All my brothers and sisters are dead, because I was the youngest of a large family, so I rely on friends. I rate friendship very highly, more so than family. One chooses one's friends. Thirty years is a very long time to live alone and life doesn't get any nicer.

© The Guardian

PATRICIA HEWITT

'Issues like childcare are political'

Patricia Hewitt is the Deputy Director of the independent left-wing think tank, the Institute for Public Policy Research, and is a member of the Labour Party's Social Justice Commission. She has two children and has written several books; the most recent, About Time, *is about revolutionising attitudes in this country towards childcare and work.*

My mother came from a family who were trained to public service and commitment to the community and she passed that spirit on to us. I was the only girl at primary school in Australia whose mother worked and even then I realised how exceptional she was and was terribly proud of her. She was always doing two or three things at once and used to quote Kipling to us about 'the unforgiving minute'. My parents were not at all political – my father was a public servant and has never told me to this day how he has voted. I became politically active at Cambridge where I started to realise I was a socialist and was passionately involved in feminist issues.

It is fascinating now for someone like me, an old lag if you like from the women's movement of twenty years ago, to look around at the new wave of women. I want to ask: 'Where are all the women like us when we were in our early twenties – fantastically politically active, making the women's movement happen, campaigning for the Sex Discrimination Act and to get women newsreaders?' It does seem as if that kind of political activism has gone right out of fashion. There is no single thing which could be called a women's liberation movement, which admittedly became quite insupportable because of all the splits and internal contradictions which drove a lot of activists off into campaigns like pro-choice, and delivering services like rape crisis centres.

Yet there *is* a new wave of feminism and I think the younger women are going to start making it happen all over again, but in a totally different way; rather than campaigning and protesting they are putting all their energies into making careers, which were not open to us in the same way, partly because we hadn't got the right qualifications but mainly because for those of us who grew up in the sixties, earning big money and having a great career wasn't where it was at.

Over half of new graduates are now women; for several years over half the lawyers graduating from university have been women, over half the accountants and nearly half the doctors. The participation rate for women without children in the work-force is just about as high as it is for men and there has been a big growth in female self-employment and in the numbers of women moving up in business and commerce. We are not seeing them yet at board level or on the bench, but women in their twenties and thirties are coming through into the middle ranks much faster and that is what is absorbing their energies in a climate where political activism seems very unattractive and unengaging.

Those women have been given no help at all, and maternity rights have actually been eroded in the past decade, but the women's liberation campaign has left behind expectations that women are going to make it. The Sex Discrimination Act did get rid of the formal barriers – for example, medical schools used to operate covert quotas against women and they actually stacked the marks so that women didn't get in, but that has gone. There are still some quite subtle forms of discrimination, like age bars – the Civil Service used to have an age bar of thirty-five which we proved was indirect discrimination because of women's different career patterns – but most professions have had to open themselves out. Moreover in a highly competitive economic environment, a lot of business leaders have now accepted what we were arguing about twenty years ago, that equal opportunities are good for business because losing highly trained women when they have children is desperately expensive in terms of re-recruiting and retraining. It is better to have paid maternity leave or a career break and get them back again.

It is that very big conflict between work and family, which still has to be tackled by women and in totally different ways. Until now the women's movement has believed that women should be competing on equal terms with men, so you get rid of the overt discrimination and then women work like men in order to get promotion. But that has meant that in order to cope with family life, those women needed twenty-four-hour substitute childcare; the idea being that the mother would see as little of her children as fathers have traditionally done, childcare would fill in the gaps and mothers would get stuck into competing and having careers and earning more money and so on. But of course that doesn't work, partly because the childcare isn't there, but much more profoundly because most women want to be with their children and some fathers would rather like to be with their children too. So the solution has to be much more revolutionary and about rethinking the balance between work, family, leisure, community activity and all the other things women do with their lives. Rather than imposing a six-hour day on everybody, we need to allow people to make different choices about how they use their time at different stages in their lives.

All the survey research shows that fulltime childcare is not the preferred option for most women. The British Social Attitudes survey asked women what childcare they would have if they could choose and they didn't say fulltime state-run nurseries, they said they wanted to be able to work, or have their partners work, the hours which enabled them to look after their children between them. There is an unmet need for nurseries, but there is a much bigger unmet need for time and we are all only just beginning to catch up with that.

I had my children very late, and when I was young I worked all hours of the day and night, starting to run a voluntary organisation and going to meetings in the evening and loving it, and that suited me fine, but now that I have small children I want to be much more flexible. I want to be able to come in much later in the morning if I have had to take a child to school and stay with him or her and I want to get home early in order to see them at that crucial time when they want to talk to me about what they have been doing. But even my work is not structured to allow that to happen and it does mean quite appalling choices.

It is possible to be a good mother and have a good career, but there are trade-offs to be made and it is high time that all employers recognised that. It makes sense for companies to offer maternity leave, a career break, term-time working or shorter hours and a lot of them are doing it. The Civil Service is doing it, IBM is doing it, many of the banks are doing it – at the moment in most cases it is only on offer for the women, but sooner or later a man is going to challenge this under the sex discrimination legislation because a career break offered exclusively to women is clearly unlawful.

The next problem is that, although it is better than what went before, more flexible arrangements will create organisations in which the people who get the really good jobs and get to the top will be the men, or the women who work like men or who have decided to have a fulltime nanny. The women who want more sensible lives may not get the really awful part-time jobs that women have had to do in the past to get the hours they needed, but they will get the middle ranking jobs and they won't be able to use their skills and talents to the extent they should. So the next challenge will be to shift part-time and flexible working much higher up the career structure – which the Civil Service is already starting to do – creating career patterns which incorporate part-time work and forcing unions and management to rethink their strategies while feminists rethink theirs.

I am very conscious of the widespread assumption that part-time work is ghettoised as bad and unskilled. Even Labour spokespeople pop up with the unemployment figures and say: 'Ah, but all the new jobs are only part-time jobs', as if it weren't a job, when in fact it is a lifeline for many women. A lot of women positively prefer part-time work, and it is not just that they don't have the choice.

I think the Labour Party needs to convey a sense of a party which has a particular view of women, work and family; that we believe women can be good mothers and good earners too, and shouldn't have to choose between the two and that fathers can be good fathers as well as good breadwinners. The Tories are so muddled on the family that they can no longer claim to be the family party. Half of them think that women should be at home with their children and half of them think they should be out working and being successful. The confusion between 'the woman at home with the children' and the 'successful high-flying woman' image means that they don't appeal to a lot of women who would like to be both those things at some stage in their lives. But it is very noticeable that in the past ten years the Tories have been head-hunting in the private sector and picking up successful women in local networks and inviting them to Conservative women's conferences and getting them involved. The Labour Party has traditionally resisted that and just expected women to show up at branch meetings which are often very off-putting.

The whole business of the 'gender gap', especially in terms of women's voting patterns at the last election, is quite fascinating. In all Labour's focus group discussions, we found that if you put a group of men and women in a room together, the men would chat away with great confidence about the world, the economy, politics and so on and the women would say: 'Oh I don't know anything about that'. Even though the levels of information were identical, the men were more confident, they felt at home with a lot of the political jargon. But when you talk to women about politics they will talk about their families. If you talk to women who haven't got children they will talk about the children they are going to have, and grandmothers talk about their grandchildren.

There is also no doubt, from all the research Labour has done, that women are much more socially responsive than men and have much higher expectations of government to act creatively to develop decent social services. Yet in voting terms it is the other way round and a lot of this seems to do with the fact that women see Labour as an intensely macho male-dominated party and they have, even more than men, very profound misgivings about us being old-fashioned extremists who would suddenly be taken over by trade unionists. At the last election they simply didn't identify good policy with Labour. Our women's ministry was quite a popular idea, but people thought it came from the Conservative Party, so instead of the good policy helping Labour's image, Labour's image meant the good policy couldn't come from it.

The encouraging thing is that we are doing so much better among younger women. In 1987 we did much better among eighteen to twenty-four-year-old women than among men in the same age group, and in 1992 we moved up and did better among the under-thirty-fives than among men in the same group, which suggests to me that we were keeping a lot of those young women; a group of people who are particularly concerned about health and education and who were much more interested in what we were saying about childcare. For the first time in 1992, childcare was coming up as an issue in its own right, which didn't happen in 1987.

I think the leadership in this area will now come from the younger women MPs who either have children themselves or have a background in feminism. Although the Tories are not delivering, they are talking about women and I do think that having a couple of female cabinet ministers will be very helpful to them. So we have to make it clear that these issues like childcare *are* political. Those largely male political journalists are not interested in them so the impetus in drawing that distinction won't come from there, but I do get the sense that the women I meet now in their twenties are not going to be content with the status quo. They are going to insist on change and the more women we get in every profession and workplace, the easier it becomes. If you have one woman in a barrister's chambers or in a serious position it is quite difficult, but if you have half a dozen it becomes easier because there is a critical mass. All these issues need to be popularised and brought into the public domain which is why women MPs are crucial and why we need to feminise our own party.

LYNNE FRANKS

*'I feel like a bird
ready to soar off'*

*Lynne Franks founded a large public relations firm in 1971. She started
her career on* Petticoat *magazine in the 1960s and her first client was the
designer Katharine Hamnett. Lynne Franks PR is now the third largest
consumer PR agency in the country. She is writing a book about her
experiences and is studying transformational psychology.*

I would describe myself as working class. My dad was a butcher
and I went to the local grammar school in north London.
Traditionally Jewish girls were then trained for marriage and
motherhood and I was the eldest of two daughters with a mother
who always wanted to be a journalist, but never really fulfilled her
own potential. It was a very matriarchal home; my maternal grandmother lived with us and my father, who was a clinical depressive,
used to come home shattered so it was always the women who kept
everything together and kept the family going. My father would
secretly have loved me to go into the butchering business, and I did
work there all through my teenage schooldays to earn my pocket
money but when I left school, with four O levels, it never occurred
to me that I wouldn't be successful and do something different.
There was never any doubt about that. Marriage and kids were not
on my agenda, but, looking back, I can see the influence of my
immigrant heritage pushing me on to be more successful in business. My grandfather came over on the boats from Russia when he

was eleven and went to work on the street markets, and I grew up with that mentality in my family although I have never really maintained the Jewish family traditions.

Public relations was still a reasonably new industry when I was young. I went to do a secretarial course when I left school and got a job in an advertising agency and then moved into the PR department by default. Then I went to work on *Petticoat*, the girl's teenage magazine, and then on to Freemans mail order company. I was in an incredible position; it was the height of the sixties and I was going to all these receptions with pop stars and fashion designers and having the time of my life. Working for the Freemans staff newspaper, interviewing men who had worked in the warehouse for fifty years on their retirement, was probably the best balance I could have had because I was living in this unreal world; an impressionable nineteen-year-old out all night with a boyfriend who worked in Carnaby Street, and working on the equivalent of a local newspaper by day.

I got into public relations after going to work for a PR in the fashion business for a couple of weeks and deciding it was quite fun because it involved talking a lot, which I always enjoyed doing. I became friends with Katharine Hamnett and she gave me the confidence to start representing her on £20 a week. I had a little second-hand typewriter and the kitchen table and a few friends from the *Petticoat* days and off we went . . . it grew quite rapidly and I got offices in Covent Garden market, more clients and more staff.

In the early seventies I got married to Paul Howie, a former Freemans colleague, and had the babies in 1976 and 1978. I was twenty-two when I started the business and the children came at a critical time; I was on a run, with the adrenalin flowing, and couldn't stop. I was a complete control freak and terribly bad at delegating. When I look back I feel I definitely sacrificed very valuable children's time and I really do regret that. Now I am over-compensating and doing the mother hen bit at a time when they are teenagers and want to spread their wings. When the business was small, I had to make the money to have help at home so I could expand. My husband was also trying to start a business so childcare wasn't a luxury – there didn't seem any other way then.

It would never have occurred to me to say: 'I am having a baby, I am really going to enjoy quality time with this child and not worry about being the biggest and best and concentrate on the real value of life because it goes very fast.' That is how I would think now but then I was thinking: 'Have the baby, get back to work, who am I going to ring?' and I actually ended up making myself ill after the second birth, learning that my body was not a machine. It is sad that you have to go through that to learn because the chances of me having another baby now are slim.

I am now in a position to think I would like to be in when the kids come home from school, but back then that wasn't the priority. I was living in south London and all our work was in the West End, and by six or seven in the evening it would never have occurred to me to go home and bath the babies. My 'masculine' energy was too high and my priorities were work, work, work instead of woman, mother, child. It is tragic that we have to sacrifice one for the other. My sister, who went to the same school as me and was brought up the same way, gave up everything to be a housewife and I used to look at her and think she was crazy, but now I don't think it at all.

I started a spiritual search about eleven years ago and became a practising Buddhist as part of a Japanese sect which involves very high energy chanting and ceremony twice a day. Life was getting out of balance and I just felt that I had no centre and that if I didn't stop soon I was going to explode. In the last couple of years I have had other spiritual searches which have helped me to understand a bit more about the eternity of life and what we are actually here on this planet to do. I do believe that we choose to be born and travel a certain path. I truly believe I chose to be born as a woman in the forties growing up post-war with all the trappings; the sixties, women's liberation, the work I am doing in communication which will take us through into the next century. I do think that the women, the mothers, are now the real hope for taking the coming generation through to the next century successfully. If we are clever enough not to die from messing up our environment and lucky enough not to blow ourselves to pieces in terrible wars and if we manage not to starve off a third of the world because of corruption, it will be the women who will teach the next generation to learn from our mistakes and to start respecting Mother Earth and not to lead this horrible selfish existence that we have done for the last fifty years. I believe the whole political and economic system, religion and marriage are going to change so quickly that even in ten years' time we are going to look back at what we grew up with and see that it is not the norm. I hope and pray that cynicism and greed will disappear.

I am always very wary of the women's movement because, although I passionately believe in the power of women, I think the moment we segregate ourselves we start to antagonise men in a way which will not help women's causes. I don't actually think it is political action which will make the changes as much as change in the home and on the streets. Segregation in any way is terribly dangerous. Good women love other women and we are able to talk to each other in a way that men never are, and I think it is through that one-to-one dialogue that the message will spread.

The media is controlled by men and there is nothing they like more than women turning into shrieking harpies that they can attack. It is a very serious job to channel all that female energy, but as a communicator I would have to think very carefully about how it should be done. Greenham, which in its heyday had a wonderful spirit, was destroyed by the way it was presented to the rest of the world. When I went there and asked why there were no men, they all said it was because when there were men there they all ended up fighting among themselves and they were non-violent people. I think that it would be very easy to put ourselves back into the mad woman stereotype and appear sexist. I think women will naturally rise up and stay up by the strength of their own individual personalities. We may not be moving as fast as we would like, but we are a hell of a lot further advanced than other industrialised countries, like Japan for example, where women know that if they want a career, they must sacrifice marriage and children. I don't think women take politics very seriously. I think they see it as being a bit childish. What we see in the House of Commons on TV *is* so childish – like little boys at school with catapults. It is always confrontational and how many women want to go into that?

I hate the way that women in business are described one way and men another. Women are much more sensitive than men and when they appear to be tougher it is not in an unfeeling way. It is using their power, their inner power, in a much more intuitive way. Of course, some women in business are worse than the men because they over-compensate, like Thatcher. I have wonderful friends who are successful, strong women for whom I have tremendous respect, but equally I have come across other women about whom I think: 'Ease up a bit, where is your humanity?' Women have to be careful not to fall into that over-compensating trap.

I don't think I would be arrogant enough to say that, as a communicator, a media person, I have any great power to make change. I think I have a responsibility as a human being to use any potential skills I have to change anything I can for the better, but I can't go around and say, 'This is the way the world has got to run.' I personally would be prepared to do whatever was needed of me to benefit the cause of women and the future generation, and there are a lot of young people in my company – men and women – who would feel the same way. We have always included a social responsibility element in our work: there are certain products we won't work for and we do try and instil an honesty policy. It is a very difficult subject because if people manufacture things, they have got to be sold and as long as you never ever lie about what you are selling, I think it is an honourable business. But, at the same time, what is the difference between lying and glamorising? Our industry is about business and business people being realistic about the bottom line.

Our business developed successfully partly because my husband and I worked together for years and were a very good balance for each other. Paul turned the business into a more disciplined company – he was logic and science and I was the emotional and creative side. I think it has worked pretty well and we do have the same feelings about things, but problems developed in our relationship. We've had twenty-odd years together and two great kids, but we both now feel the need for change and freedom from each other. There has been a competitive element and it is very hard for me to analyse why I am no longer with him; I can only say that it feels right and it isn't at all sad. I always had such a fear of being on my own and it hasn't been easy coming to terms with that, but somewhere there must have been a real subconscious strain because I feel now like my heart has been freed up. I am forty-four, I have built up a business I am proud of, but I am in a position where I can expand into other areas if I choose to. My children are in their teens and I now wish to be their friend as much as anything else. I feel like a bird ready to soar off.

I don't quite know where I will go but I feel it will be an area with a spiritual element, with health and healing. I wouldn't label myself Buddhist any more. I think that was all part of not having the courage just to be Lynne Franks. I hate the fact that the company has my name because it makes me so high profile, and now I want to move on with the experience and the knowledge of the last twenty years, but not with the baggage. I want to start with a very blank page.

I am now thinking small and precious. In five years from now I know I won't be living a stressed-out business life, because I think I would be wasting whatever potential I have.

I feel passionately that women shouldn't make the same mistakes as men and wake up at sixty-five and say: 'I have just sacrificed my family and my life and what am I going to do now?' You see these men, these ex-chief execs or company chairmen, pushing the supermarket trolley around with their wives and they are just ready to die. They have lived their lives. I don't think that women should fall into that trap. I have seen how easy it is, having sacrificed my own relationship with my kids when they were little and I wish I had worked out a way of balancing more. Maybe if I had worked from home or I had managed to live nearer to the office; things that

I didn't think about at the time because I wanted to live in the nicest possible environment even if it meant that I didn't come home very often. Women absolutely mustn't make the same mistakes as men. It is not the outward symbols of success – the chauffeur-driven cars, the position, the name on the door of the office – that count. It is about balance and compromise – and not finding that out too late.

CERILAN ROGERS

'Starting out
in medicine is like
being thrown into
the trenches'

*Cerilan Rogers comes from a South Wales mining family and is the
daughter of a Labour MP. She trained and worked as a general
practitioner and is the mother of three small boys. She is now studying
public health in North Wales.*

Why did I decide to become a doctor? This will sound corny, but
it's true – my grandfather had pneumoconiosis and, like many in
the South Wales mining valleys, our family relied a great deal on
the doctor. Doctors were widely respected in the community – this
was of course after 1948 and people felt they owned the National
Health Service in the same way as many had initially felt they
owned the Coal Board. The pits and the health service were theirs
and there was a lot of pride in that. My grandfather would have
loved to have been a doctor himself. He had been down the pit
all his life and was ill for most of mine, so the doctor was a central
figure in our lives. I didn't know my father's parents, they had died
before I was born, but I was very close to my mother's parents.

When I was fifteen, I didn't want to go to university at all. I
ended up at Cambridge, thanks to a rather forceful headmistress
who persuaded me to sit Cambridge entrance after I had messed up
my A levels and failed to get the right grades for Bart's. I didn't
want to resit physics and chemistry, which I hated, and was able
to leave school when Cambridge accepted me. I didn't like the

physical sciences at all, I just wanted to be a doctor. Cambridge was a very different environment to South Wales! I eventually came to terms with it, and myself, but it took some time.

Everyone expected me to be political because my father, who is now a Labour MP, was so involved in local politics, but I think I would have been anyway – South Wales was that sort of place when I grew up. The contrast with Cambridge just finished the process. We very rarely talked politics as such at home when I was a child. I don't remember ever being sat down and told what to think. There was no pressure to conform; we all used to help at elections which were great fun. I joined the Labour Party when I was fifteen and have never regretted it. I quite often disagree with aspects of policy and don't always see eye to eye with my father, but it isn't a problem. My parents brought us up to think for ourselves; the fact that we often agree with them is a tribute to their good sense! I was very active politically before I had my children, but it is much more difficult to find the time now.

I entered the medical profession at a time when it was beginning to change. When I went to Cambridge there were only six colleges that accepted women. Now there is a 50 per cent female intake into medical school. However, there is still more subtle, indirect discrimination. The system itself discriminates against women. Training in hospital medicine means moving around a lot, you really need to be mobile to get on, which is hard if you have a family. Men have to move their families too, but their wives usually sacrifice their careers. If you marry a doctor, you have to balance the demands of two careers. I went into general practice for three reasons: I could work within a community, I was able to stay in one area because all the training posts were linked and I wasn't keen enough on hospital medicine to spend the rest of my life in it. I was already established as a GP when I married, but I had to leave my practice when my husband, also a doctor, had to move to North Wales.

Women tend not to go into the 'glamour' specialities, which are mainly the surgical ones. There is a lot of competition for the good training jobs and it's hard to climb the ladder and have a family. There are very few female consultants in general surgery, obstetrics and gynaecology and orthopaedics. These are incidentally where the big money can be made in private practice. General surgery is also seen as being quite macho, exciting stuff. You are not endlessly involved in insoluble problems; you remove the problem and if you can't, it's not a surgical problem and someone else has to deal with it.

Many women are attracted to general practice, partly because of the nature of the work, but also because of the relatively short period of hospital training. You can be a principal in general practice four years after qualifying as a doctor, and very few consultants are that young. Part-time work is also available. But it's a fallacy to think that general practice is an easy option. You have nights and weekends on call when you are the first point of contact for the patient. If you are part-time, your contribution is often undervalued in financial terms. Many women GPs feel their remuneration does not reflect the value of their work. The problem of violence towards doctors is also a growing concern and GPs are in the front line. Women are particularly vulnerable, although men are also at risk.

In South Wales I worked fulltime, but did genetics as well as general practice. When I moved to North Wales, I took a fulltime post in general practice, and I now work fulltime in public health medicine. I don't regret always having worked fulltime. I have three boys, all under the age of six, but I don't feel I have made any sacrifices. I have the best of both worlds, all the pleasure of the children and the enjoyment of a good career. I pay out a lot on childcare, but I'm luckier than most women as I can afford it.

Having the babies was the most difficult time. GPs are self-employed and arrangements for maternity leave are up to individuals. I had to pay for my own locum cover during my second pregnancy and had to go back to work when the baby was only eight weeks old. The government had changed the rules by the time I had my third baby, so I had some help with the locum payments. I feel very strongly that women GPs should have the same rights to maternity leave as other women in public sector services. Independent contractor status is the excuse for not allowing this, but I can't believe it is beyond the wit of man to find a way around it. The problem is that it *is* the wit of man and maternity leave is not a high priority for most men. A major asset for me has been a brilliant husband, who is both willing and able to do his full share of parenting.

Many of the changes in attitude and practice, which would improve the lot of women doctors, would also improve life for their male colleagues. I think there have been changes, partly due to the greater numbers of women qualifying, but there is still a long way to go. Personally, the only time I have felt disadvantaged in my professional life by my sex was during my pregnancies, but it was a very unpleasant experience and I felt bitter for some time.

Starting out in medicine is a bit like being thrown into the trenches. My first job as a medical house officer was the worst experience of my life. I had a busy job, which included coronary care, and worked every day and every other night and every other weekend – 108 hours a week. We had two weeks' holiday in six months. When I came home on holiday, I passed a pelican crossing which went off while I was walking past and I was so confused I thought it was my cardiac arrest bleep! Utter panic! I felt shell-shocked and desperately tired. You end up resenting patients because they represent more work. It is a dreadful situation, which is only now changing with the new regulations on junior doctors' hours. Junior medical staff have put up with it for years, because they are totally dependent on their seniors for references. Also the short-term contracts give you no job security. Many consultants regarded the long hours as important elements of training, having forgotten or chosen to forget their own experiences. Medical advances have changed the nature of the work for junior doctors; they are required to do much more for their patients and the pressure is correspondingly greater, particularly in areas such as neo-natal medicine. Some older consultants simply don't appreciate the pressure. Many of the younger consultants are much more sympathetic, but the main thrust for change has come from junior doctors themselves, helped by an increasingly litigious public. Any lawyer worth his salt will look at how long a doctor has been on duty if a mistake has been made.

Another issue is how well the medical profession serves women generally. I think the situation here is a reflection of the way society treats women. On the whole, their needs are often unrecognised or given low priority. Men don't really understand women and male doctors aren't a notable exception. There is clear evidence that women's symptoms are more often considered to be psychological than are men's and they are more likely to be diagnosed as suffering from depression or anxiety. What most of them need is a change in their lives; they need decent housing, decent childcare and education, decent levels of income. Doctors can't provide these, but in modern society there is often no one else to turn to. I often used to come home at the end of the day thinking 'I'm not a doctor, I'm a priest.' People's circumstances and experiences are powerful determinants of their health, so to that extent they are the legitimate concern of doctors, but many doctors are reluctant to tackle these issues because they feel so powerless to bring about change. Women bear the burden of care for their families and are the first to feel the effects of worsening social conditions.

I changed to public health medicine partly because of my dissatisfaction with the new GP contract. I felt we were being dictated to as regards the content of our work. I felt there was little point in screening our elderly patients when our ability to respond to the needs we uncovered was being curtailed by cuts in social services. Public health gives you more opportunity to consider the broader view. It is a bit like being a general practitioner only the whole population is your patient and your responsibility. You have to determine the needs of your population and how best to meet those needs. Anything which affects health is a legitimate concern, so all the social factors have to be considered. The effect of poverty and stress on health was most powerfully brought home to me during the miners' strike when I was still in general practice. I knew many families who were desperately trying to keep their lives together and for many it has been downhill ever since. If you are unemployed, it is much harder to eat, keep your house warm, survive. My husband sees children whose hands and feet are blue with cold, despite having waited in a relatively warm waiting area, because they have come from a cold home. There is a lot of 'victim blaming' these days, which is the inevitable result of the current emphasis on individual responsibility. But when you have no control over circumstances, like unemployment, the notion of individual responsibility becomes a sick joke.

Looking around you can't fail to notice that times are hard. People look poorer, there are more people sleeping rough, many of them obviously in poor mental health. It is appalling, but even small actions can make a difference to individuals. Doctors may feel powerless, but their decisions can have a major impact on their patients' lives. Collectively they could be a very powerful force for good, if they accepted they had a responsibility for health and not just for sickness. There are a lot of concerned and caring doctors who have survived the brutality of their training, but it is difficult to speak out in medicine and to challenge the establishment. There is a price to pay for being too political. You run the risk of being marginalised and of provoking a 'there she goes again' reaction. They don't hear the message if they think they are hearing dogma, they just switch off.

There is a danger these days that very real and potentially dangerous deficiencies in services will occur because NHS staff are afraid to speak out. The NHS is undergoing major upheaval and doctors must monitor these changes and the effect they have on patients and, where there are problems, be brave enough to speak out. Many have in the past and I hope that those who do in the future will find themselves supported by the rest of us. I'm enough of an optimist to think they will.

CATE HASTE

'Abortion was the key politicising issue for women'

Cate Haste is a writer and television producer/director. Her last book, Rules of Desire, *is a history of sex in Britain since the First World War.*

I wrote *Rules of Desire* because I wanted to look not so much at sexual behaviour but at how the rules which govern and control sexual behaviour, and which tend to be synonymous with controlling women, have changed. I was brought up in a generation in which women were expected to get married and have a family. But my mother was a teacher and both my parents believed girls were as capable as boys, so my horizons were extended already, and I never believed that marriage was my sole lot in life.

A lot of my political awakening in the late fifties and sixties, on CND marches and so on, was tied in with a sense that women could expect more for their lives. There was also a feeling then that there was a desperate need for a change in sexual values, and that the laws on homosexuality, abortion, divorce and censorship were unjust, hypocritical and downright archaic. It was one aspect of a wider mood for change and regeneration. The Labour government liberalised those laws in the 1960s. When I was writing the book, it became clear that those reforming politicians were then in their middle age, and I began to wonder where they got *their* ideas from. As I researched, I began to see that changes which appeared to be dramatic in the sixties had started at an earlier point.

That point was just before the First World War, with the transition from the Victorians to the Edwardians and all the social upheaval and change that went along with that. There was a questioning of the hypocrisy of sexual standards governing public and private life on the one hand, which included plays like George Bernard Shaw's *Mrs Warren's Profession* and Ibsen's *Ghosts*, and there were the sex psychologists like Freud and Havelock Ellis who were looking at sex in a totally new way, freeing it from the old taboos.

The suffrage movement was very important – the impetus which came from the political fight for the vote made women start thinking about their personal emancipation. Was emancipation only about the vote, or was it about education and employment opportunities and women's role in the family – and was it also about their sexuality? Younger women began to link personal emancipation with sexual freedom. Birth control had been available to the middle classes for over twenty years. But whereas older feminists thought birth control benefited only men (by removing the penalties of 'fornication'), younger feminists like Dora Russell began to see it as an agent of their own emancipation because it meant they could take control of their lives.

As the shocking details began to emerge during the First World War of the conditions in which women engaged in childbirth and child-rearing, there was a point around which women could organise. It was largely a middle-class movement, directed at improving the nation's health. Women's health and maternal and infant mortality were looked at in particular, and local government mother and baby clinics were set up in 1918. However the maternal morbidity rate remained high, and part of the reason was attributed to illegal abortion. Over five hundred of an estimated 150,000 women who resorted to ghastly illegal abortions died each year in the late 1930s.

Abortion wasn't picked up politically or in legislation until the 1960s and 1970s and, in terms of feminism, it was probably the key politicising issue for women. Defending a woman's right to choose against the various amendments to the Abortion Act in the seventies was fantastically important in galvanising women.

In those early days Marie Stopes's crusade to provide working-class women with birth control facilities attracted enormous hostility. She was attacked for using the poor for experiments, and there was a strong body of opinion which said birth control was a right for middle-class women but once it was available to the working class then the 'floodgates of immorality' would be opened; where would it all end if the penalties on sex were removed? It was a class snobbery which ran all through sexual issues – like pornography being prosecuted if it was cheap but allowed if it was expensive – until the democratisation of sex in the seventies. But the early debate about birth control also resulted in a distinction being drawn between a moral and a medical issue. People began to see sex in terms of health, not morality.

Most sex reformers in the twenties and thirties were concerned to educate people basically not only about their health, but also about women's right to enjoy sex. The information coming from the women at the birth control clinics suggested that they didn't think they could enjoy sex. It wasn't something they participated in with pleasure, it was something they endured with the fear every time that a child might follow.

There were women like Marie Stopes saying birth control should be available to all, and also women like Dr Helena Wright saying women should be taught that they had the ability to enjoy sex without shame and that actually meant getting to know their bodies, examining and discussing their bodies and experimenting. It also meant communicating with their husbands and making love which led to mutual pleasure and mutual orgasm.

The pill was really the icing on the cake – it wasn't the thing which drove women suddenly into bed but with the risk of pregnancy reduced, it enabled the flowering of the whole area of sexuality. By the sixties, sexual issues were being addressed as issues of public policy. They hadn't been politicised until then, however, because sex was still seen as too embarrassing, a vote-loser and a non-party issue, which tended to be discussed in hushed tones in public and dressed up in lots of euphemisms. That has actually survived in many women over sixty now when they talk about sex.

I think the pill had a wider impact on women's lives. Once they felt they had sexual and erotic equality, they started to ask why they hadn't got equality in terms of opportunities and employment. In my own profession, television, I was active on the ACTT equality committee, which produced quite a radical report, 'Patterns of Discrimination', in the 1970s showing how women were ghettoised in low paid, lower status jobs. Because there was equal pay, people could argue there was no discrimination against women. But there were very few women indeed then in top jobs and we all knew it was more difficult for women than for men to get on.

Women weren't taken as seriously as men, they were OK in servicing jobs but not in the really responsible ones, and those who were producers or directors had to fight against a lot of male prejudice and *never* make mistakes. Think what a brouhaha there was over the first woman newsreader, Anna Ford, and how few women there were anywhere on 'serious' television, even in the early 1980s. There has been a gradual change since then, largely because women spoke up for themselves and organised to get their views heard. It's unlikely today that a man would ask a woman in an interview, as I was asked only ten years ago, how she could cope with a job and children. Nobody would have asked a man that. The independent sector has opened a lot more doors for women, so there has been some progress, but if you look at the management of, for instance, the new ITV companies they're almost all men in some version of a grey suit.

A less welcome side-effect of sexual liberation has been that, while the moral opprobrium and ostracism which used to be heaped on women who got pregnant without being married has gone, women who become single parents still have a very difficult time. The fact that there are no rules any more has in some ways been to the detriment of women. They've been led to believe that they have the choice in how to live their lives and make relationships, but the practical consequences for single mothers can be dire. Though many single mothers want to earn a decent wage as the sole bread-winners, it's still the case that women get paid much less than men and are still clustered in the low paid jobs. Provision for childcare is abysmal and the jobs mothers can do with small children are limited. Over half get no maintenance and most find themselves on social security unable to get off it and falling into the 'poverty trap'. There is no incentive to retrain or work even though many want to be economically self-sufficient.

Ironically this coincided with a political debate centred on 'family values' in the 1980s. The Thatcher and Tebbit government evoked the spectre of 'permissiveness' – a sort of political bogey-man – as the price of the return of a Labour government, while they claimed to be making all sorts of attempts to support family life. But what actually happened during the eighties was that, with rising unemployment, benefit cuts and care being handed to the community, families, particularly poorer families, got even less support. Meanwhile there was a rapid acceleration in all classes of every single indicator of 'permissive' behaviour – co-habitation, pre-marital sex, children born outside marriage, divorce. Far from returning to Victorian values, people are signalling that they enjoy their freedom and want to keep it. I don't see any sign that we are going back to 'traditional values' at the moment.

Today most sexual issues are amenable to political discussion, you can see that in the discussion around AIDS. An enormous amount of prejudice from people who did not want to discuss sexual behaviour had to be overcome. The health education campaigns admitted that we are in a society where most people have sexual experience with several partners before marriage, and obviously for Christian fundamentalists and moral groups that was very difficult. In addition, there was an unprecedented amount of explicit detail in promoting safer sex, justified by the fact that an epidemic was threatened. So most taboos that were left about public discussion of sex evaporated, at least temporarily. But the panic around AIDS also brought out a nastier side with an increase in homophobia. There had been a consistent shift towards tolerance of different sexualities, but now there's been a shift back – there's some pressure to have homosexual activity criminalised again, for example, and for homosexuals to be barred from teaching, which is the old moral right rearing its horns again.

In the late 1960s and 1970s people came to believe sex was healthy and to be explored as part of self-awareness and growth. Women bought into this new freedom, but for feminists it was also about redefining women's sexuality and sexual desires on their own terms, not men's, and claiming that our bodies are our own. There has again been a change because sex can't be seen as unequivocally healthy when there's the threat of HIV. So there are new rules for both men and women.

PRAGNA PATEL
'We have to encourage women to take up their rights'

Pragna Patel is one of the Southall Black Sisters, a group from West London founded in 1979 to campaign on behalf of Asian and Afro-Caribbean women and to provide advice and shelter for women who are victims of domestic violence. In 1992, following three years of hard campaigning with other women's groups, they secured the release of Kiranjit Ahluwhalia, a battered wife, from prison. As a result of this and their history of campaigning, they were awarded the Martin Ennals Civil Liberties award in recognition of 'their out-standing contribution towards the furtherance of civil liberties and human rights.'

This group was started by women who had been active fighting racism at an institutional level, as well as on the streets, for some time. Because of a lot of National Front activity in this area in the late 1970s, there was a generally heightened awareness of racism and the younger generation of black people felt the need to forge some kind of positive identity for themselves, as people who were going to live here for the rest of their lives. The group was formed soon after the 1979 race riots in which Blair Peach died and a huge number of black people were injured and arrested. Large numbers of Asian youths were being criminalised by the police and the National Front were being allowed to march through the area and hold public meetings. The Anti-Nazi League was also active in a big way, which popularised anti-racism among the youth. Some black women became concerned and uncomfortable about the fact that gender was never discussed as an issue within anti-racist political groups. They felt it was being dismissed, as was the way in which black women's lives were shaped in this country, so they formed the Southall Black Sisters.

In this day and age that name may sound like an anachronism, but at that time there was this awareness about being black and about turning black into a positive term – the phrase 'Black is Beautiful' was much in use. There was a need to derive some kind of power from turning the whole thing on its head and reforging a kind of black identity. At the same time feminism was growing, and women were beginning to come together and look at themselves in a kind of sisterhood.

We started off developing the analysis of gender in relationship to black women – and that hasn't changed. What has changed is the political perspective. The early group campaigned around a number of issues, particularly around issues to do with racism and the unionisation of black women. The group supported the women's rights to join a union and they were also involved in homelessness campaigns and campaigns to do with the immigration laws and nationality. They fought the virginity tests by immigration officers on Asian women, for example – a particularly racist, sexist act enforced to try and prove that if Asian women were bona fide fiancées then they would be virgins before they came to this country. The turning point for the Southall Black Sisters in terms of gender issues was the case of a local woman who was killed by her husband and an accomplice he had hired to set fire to the house. She died in that fire along with three of her five daughters. Two managed to escape and were placed in foster care, but the others were killed by him purely because he was angry that she didn't give birth to sons. The community, which was highly politicised around the race issue, responded with silence. Nobody protested that it was an outrage which shouldn't be tolerated. It was left to the Southall Black Sisters to raise it and that was the beginning of us looking at issues affecting women within the community in a very raw way.

*

It has been twelve years since then and we have been forced to confront many other issues. From early on, the group faced a lot of hostility from every single quarter of the community. They faced hostility from the conservative and orthodox elements – the religious institutions and the Indian Workers' Association, which were entirely male-dominated and thought that women's issues didn't exist – they denounced the Southall Black Sisters as lunatic feminists. The left, which was dominated by young Asian men, many of whom were extremely sexist and didn't involve women in their groups, were also particularly hostile. Some members of the Southall Black Sisters got individual threats from certain members of the Southall Youth Movement, an Asian youth organisation, so there was a very hostile environment in which they were trying to develop politics that reflected the experiences of black or Asian women.

Feminism was generally awakening at the same time, but there were fractures within the feminist organisations, over issues such as sexuality and all that obviously had an effect on the politics of feminism. When feminists talked, did we know who they were talking about? Which interests were they reflecting? Black women around the country were coming together to see if there could be a national organisation for black women. But the first conference led to splits and fractures because there were all these other identities wanting to have a say. Early SBS women were much more inclined towards radical feminism – a separatist feminism which advocated that you just couldn't work with men. That grew partly out of their real experience of working with men and finding that, again and again, the issues to do with women were being sidelined and trivialised. That, however, has changed.

When SBS first set up a black women's centre in Southall, there was a big debate as to whether we should be up-front about our politics, because we were worried that if we said we are Southall Black Sisters, standing for a kind of radical, alternative programme for women, would women come to us? Would they be allowed to come by their husbands? Would they identify with the group? The alternative was to have a bland name, not to be very public about our politics and to organise activities that would be safe in the eyes of the community. By safe I mean issues that wouldn't be threatening to the community – like English classes, sewing and traditional activities that women might be allowed to take part in. In the end we took the step of being open and public and saying that we would offer advice on a range of issues, including violence to women, domestic violence, rape and sexual harassment.

We didn't know the direction in which we were going and we didn't really know what issues women would bring to us – they could have been to do with employment or with immigration, education or homelessness. What we have found over the years is that most of the women who come to us, and obviously the majority are Asian women because it is a predominantly Asian community, come with problems of violence. It wasn't that we plucked it out of the air and decided that was what we were going to do. Over the years we have developed very strong case-work experience including advocacy, counselling and advice work around issues to do with domestic violence, incest, sexual abuse, sexual harassment and so on. As part of that we obviously have to deal with homelessness, social security and, more recently, immigration complications where women have to face violence.

We were initially branded with the image of home wreckers by the conservative elements in the community, which was inevitable. Meanwhile the progressive groups were accusing us of raising all these issues and exposing our internal problems to the white community, thereby inviting a racist backlash in which the media could depict all Asian families as pathological. It is true that we are lifting the lid, but what are we supposed to do? We must confront racism, but it is not the only thing that shapes our lives as women and if women are being oppressed and harassed within the family we have to raise these issues and make demands.

A lot of our campaigns involve white women and that has been vital to us because domestic violence is not just an issue for the Asian community, it is a universal phenomenon and not specific to any culture, religion or country. The difference is that with Asian women, the cultural factors influence how women respond to that violence. Asian culture is not the cause of the violence itself – we have exploded that myth – but there are certain factors, certain aspects in Asian family life – though this is not uniform – which make it difficult for women to deal with and escape that violence. I would refer specifically to issues like the code of honour. That is not just specific to Asian communities generally, it is also prevalent in some Latin American, Mediterranean and Palestinian communities. It is a very male concept which means that the family, or the wider community group to which a family belongs, has to guard its honour. That honour rests on women's behaviour and if women deviate from their prescribed role and position, they are seen to be staining the honour of the family or bringing disgrace to the family.

The social consequences of this are very grave in terms of isolation from the community and stigma for the women, children or other members of the family. That makes it extremely difficult for Asian women to get away from violent relationships or to leave their marriages. A lot of our work at the centre involves counselling women around this concept and trying to encourage women not to look at what others will do or say, but to look at their needs and their children's needs. Their physical and mental well-being should come first.

People forget that what we experience and how women negotiate violence is so much affected by the culture in which we live. That feeling of shame and having failed in a marriage is universal because marriage is an institution which many women are socialised into believing should be their life. That is particularly true for Asian women.

We have four workers at the moment and we can't cope with the demands. I just wonder where the women go in other Asian communities where there are no centres like ours. To give an example, one of our workers is in court this morning helping an Asian woman who came to us for help because her husband was being violent and abusive. Also he wasn't reliable. She wasn't sure when the money was coming in, he wasn't taking any responsibility, she got really depressed and earlier this week the police rang us up saying she had just tried to jump on to the rails at Southall station. They have gone to court this morning to try to get an injunction to have the husband removed from the house – which won't be easy because the grounds are mental rather than physical cruelty, and it is much harder to get the courts to accept this. We often get demands from as far afield as Tower Hamlets, as well as our neighbouring boroughs where centres like ours don't exist. There are a lot of other women's centres, but they are not necessarily radical in any way. They often reinforce traditional values and fail to offer women alternatives. Instead they are often sent back into the home to try and work things out and invited to bring their husbands or fathers in, so things can be 'resolved amicably'. We don't have a policy of reconciliation. We are not Relate. Our job is not marriage guidance – it is to help women deal with violence and abuse, to help them realise they shouldn't tolerate it and to show them there are certain rights to which they are entitled. We have to encourage women to take up those rights.

We are not saying: 'Break up your family', but these are women with problems and the last thing they want to be told is to go back home. Most of the women who come here come as a last resort: they know how strong the feeling of isolation will be if they leave their family because it will mean leaving their community. For black and minority women it is even harder because the outside world is unknown to them. They may not speak English, they don't know their way around, they don't know how to deal with institutions or how to get money to live on. Even if they can speak English they are often afraid of being subjected to racial attacks. We have cases where single Asian women, who have left violent husbands, have been subjected to racist attacks and have returned to violent husbands because it is the better of the two evils.

They also need practical help in the form of emergency payments, housing, getting their belongings from their homes, finding interpreters, legal advice, having someone to go to court with them. It is amazing how few solicitors offer interpretation.

Unravelling the mess and the bureaucracy is half our battle, because solicitors work so tightly on legal aid that they will give a very limited amount of their time and that is often not enough if the women are to be reassured and helped to feel confident. So we do a lot of the back-up work, clarifying what the solicitors have said and so on. It has got to such a state that solicitors often rely on us to debrief the women and collect the evidence necessary to make sure the whole story is there.

Dealing with the police is another nightmare. We don't even have a domestic violence unit in Southall, an area which might as well not have heard about the wider police initiatives on domestic violence. We are constantly filing complaints to the police for failing to really help women. Interpretation at police stations can sometimes increase the difficulties. They rely on a few Asian male interpreters who are not trained or very sympathetic to the issue of domestic violence and who are often personally identified with the police.

We are also tearing our hair out about immigration law. We have several domestic violence cases at the moment, not all Asian women, whose immigration status is dependent entirely on their husband's. That means they are entrapped in violent situations. If they leave the marriage, they are liable to be deported. So they stay within violent relationships and risk their lives. That is one of the most difficult problems for us because when they come to us, we just don't know what to do. They cannot claim any form of public assistance or benefits due to immigration rules and regulations. We can't send them to refuges because who is going to pay their rent? That kind of racism has to be addressed.

All these factors and pressures come into play in making decisions about what to do with most of those women. Because they have been inculcated with certain values about their position within the family, it also means they have a hard time trying to conceive of themselves living on their own. Many have had arranged marriages, have moved from their parents' family into another family and they have never lived by themselves. So it is daunting for them to suddenly make the decision to leave. One of the first avenues they will choose is reconciliation and that means bringing together influential members of the family – respected members of the community – to try to resolve the problem. Women who come to us have told us time and time again how reconciliation has been tried and failed because they don't have the power to enforce decisions. And in any case in such meetings they are not believed. They are told if their husbands are violent, maybe it is their fault for nagging and maybe they should stop nagging. So the last thing they want to hear when they come to us is: 'Go back and try again – or let us bring in somebody to discuss your problems.' They want some kind of practical help. We try to see things all the way through and once the women are settled, we try to involve them in the centre. They usually come with their children and are homeless, but we have very good links with Asian women's refuges ourselves. It is amazing how many come here, frightened and vulnerable, thinking they are the only ones – and we see hundreds of women every year – so it is important to try and send them somewhere where they can see other women, who speak the same language, going through the same experience.

There are other Asian women who speak excellent English and who have been born, brought up and educated here and they may prefer a mixed refuge. Some women want to stay in the locality and other women want to get far away – to the north of England maybe. Our aim is to give them a choice, an alternative, not to force them to leave their home but to support them if that is what they want. We have to say to them: 'These are your choices and you shouldn't feel ashamed about taking these routes.'

VERITY
LAMBERT

*'In the right place
at the right time'*

*Verity Lambert has been a television producer for over thirty years.
She started producing Dr Who at twenty-six, became Head of Drama
at Thames Television and ran Euston Films. She now runs her own
company, Cinema Verity, in west London.*

The way that successful women are talked about by the media is
very sexist; adjectives like 'tough' and 'ruthless' are used and
always in a pejorative sense. They never say 'firm' or 'forward-
looking'. The sub-text is that if you are a woman who has her own
opinions, somehow or other that is not quite right.

I would not attribute my success to toughness or ruthlessness. I
plead guilty to being in the right place at the right time in the early
sixties when women producers and directors in my particular area
were very few and far between. I was lucky to have worked with
Sidney Newman at ABC who then moved to the BBC as Head of
Drama and thought of me for *Dr Who*. I know that the success of
Dr Who, to a certain extent, had something to do with luck because
I didn't really know about producing, although I did have a certain
amount of judgement, instinct and taste, which probably carried
me through. After that beginning, it wasn't all due to luck; anyone
who believes that can't really have much faith in their own ability.

I think to a certain extent I am no different to any other viewer.
I want to be entertained, I enjoy popular entertainment and I am

not a particularly high-brow person, so I think I have an instinct about what people who watch popular drama want. One of the things I think about is whether ideas are based in some kind of reality, so that people are exposed to experiences which illuminate and reflect society. A lot of the best television, even if it is humorous, works because it reflects life in this country today.

The original format and intention of *Minder*, which I suppose would be looked on as totally popular entertainment, was to take a look at ethnic minorities in an urban environment. The creator, Leon Griffiths, chose two characters who in turn would reflect various points of view. The really clever thing about it was that you recognised the Arthur Daley character – the bigoted pseudo-respectable person who wanted to be a Kray brother but didn't have a nasty enough streak or the smartness to be that bad, with 'her indoors' as a wife and very definite attitudes towards sex and certain minorities – but the Terry character, who the viewer expected to be much more like that, was in fact the liberal. In that way we exposed prejudice as being silly and turned it on its head.

The shows which I have been most proud of have been those which have had a very definite message but have also been popular enough to reach millions of people. Shows like *The Naked Civil Servant*, about Quentin Crisp – somebody who was prepared to be honest about himself and prepared to stand up and be counted for what he was, a gay man, at a time when it was very difficult to do that. The interesting thing was that, although it was outrageous and funny, we only got three complaints and hundreds of letters and phone calls from people who said they had changed their views on gays. I think it's great if you can make people re-assess their attitudes without hitting them on the head with the message.

Two series stand out very distinctly to me as carrying a powerful message about women. The first was *Shoulder to Shoulder** of which I am very proud and which came out of a relationship

---

**Shoulder to Shoulder* was a television series about the lives of Emmeline Pankhurst and her two daughters Christabel and Sylvia.

between Georgia Brown, the lifelong feminist Midge Mackenzie and myself. We put the idea to the BBC after researching it and forming a small company to make it. Most importantly I learned something from it because, although I had been taught something about women's emancipation at school, it had been very cursory. The only thing I really remembered was that there were these women who chained themselves to railings and threw themselves in front of horses; that summed up my knowledge regarding women winning the right to vote.

It raised my own consciousness about women and the women's movement and I hope put it forward in an entertaining, moving and illuminating manner. Viewers felt they were involved in a struggle and, at the end of it, could really tell what the different factions were and why certain things were done. We had many letters from women who hadn't realised what had gone into getting the vote, some who had never voted and said they would never not vote again, because they realised what had gone into their enfranchisement. *Shoulder to Shoulder* opened my eyes to the women's movement.

Another example of a series in which women were the main protagonists was Euston Films' *Widows*. I was working with Linda Agran and we both felt it was not right that we were making male-dominated series. I felt we had to make a show about women in which they were the central characters. (I was also running Thames' drama at the time and we came up with Antonia Fraser's *Jemima Shaw* there). Then this wonderful idea came in from Lynda La Plante about women whose husbands had died in a robbery. Here were these women who had come from probably the most male-dominated strata of society, who never inquired what their husbands did, who lived in a total male-dominated enclave. Suddenly and tragically, they lose all their husbands. One of them decides that she is not going to go back to being naïve and protect-ed, she is going to take control of her own life. So she takes over. It was extremely entertaining, and one of the reasons that women really enjoyed the series was that it showed them making a change and controlling their lives.

*

I am a feminist, I am not part of any club. There is only one man working here in my offices – not because I sat down and said: 'I must employ women', but because instinctively I feel that when women come in and have something to offer, they are just so good. I believe there is a residue of subconscious sexism which will never really go, which results from the way we are taught in schools from an early age and Pavlovian reactions are set up. I have them; I will always go to do the washing up, not because anyone is telling me to do it, but because it is an instinctive reaction.

I don't think it has been especially tough for me being a woman. I was offered an opportunity to produce *Dr Who* at twenty-six. That was very young, even for a man, in those days. I was the youngest producer in the drama department and much the youngest woman. Without that I would have got out of the business. I had already given myself a year to move up from being a production assistant. In some ways there are more opportunities now and in some ways less. The training and the structure in which people went into the business, trained, got jobs and were protected has gone for both men and women. Although it is still a male-dominated industry, there is a much larger independent sector, and because women have had to operate in a rather less structured manner, they are perhaps more suited to that. I can't say I feel very optimistic about broadcasting generally. It is going to be very, very commercial, programmes are going to be required to perform, there will be less opportunity to let things sit there and grow. If *Minder* were to hit the airwaves now it would probably not last because in its first series it didn't do that well. I think that Sky is going to be extremely successful and start making money and it will make it very difficult for ITV to avoid going downhill. I don't know if anyone has got the bottle to try and stop that and if the BBC goes, that will be a total and utter disaster – a national tragedy.

I formed my own company because, after many many years of working within a corporate structure, I could see that the freedom that I had as a producer and as a head of department was going. I had the best years at Thames and Euston working for Jeremy Isaacs and Brian Cargill – very different people but both programme makers who understood about instinct and let me get on with it. Then I had three years in the feature film industry at Thorn EMI which were the most miserable of my life. Everyone second guessed everyone else and it just drove me insane – I couldn't do any good work there. When I came out I had a real think about life and whether I should go back into the corporate structure and do what I enjoy doing most, which is producing. Running my own company I can have the freedom to have a little more control, although in the end I still have to sell it to someone.

I was married for ten years and we decided not to have children. I suppose, to be very honest, I don't think I am a very maternal person – certainly by the time I had to think finally about children in a serious way I had stopped being maternal at all, so it wasn't what some people would call a sacrifice. But I think the way I work, which is quite obsessively, might have made motherhood difficult.

DOUNNE ALEXANDER

'Judged as a black single parent with all the stereotypical images'

Dounne Alexander was born in Trinidad and moved to Britain in her teens. She has two daughters and now runs her own small business, Gramma's UK Ltd, making and marketing her unique Caribbean herbal pepper sauces in Essex.

I was born very prematurely with severe breathing and digestive problems and my maternal grandmother was my lifeline. I was closer to her than to anyone else I have ever come across on this earth. She kept me alive with this very special product, this herbal pepper sauce, her recipe for which I now make and sell. She was always giving, sharing and loving and she didn't see any evil in anyone, but looking back now I think she was very angelic and revolutionary for an uneducated woman. My father's side of the family were very eminent, educated people. My paternal grandfather ran his own private school whereas my mother's side were poor country folk and it was fascinating to compare folk education (based on wisdom) with real education (based on books) because there was such a colossal difference between the two. All the warmth, the time and the patience was on the side of the country folk, to whom I always felt closer than the city folk. My grandmother always saw a deeper meaning to life and would tell me, when I was a small child, that the secrets she was giving me then would be used by me in later life and now it is all coming together. She taught me that everyone had spiritual powers, but that those powers were more developed in some people than others. She died when I was thirteen, but she left me her wisdom and many special recipes, including this herbal pepper sauce which contains thirty different digestible herbs and spices, as her legacy. You can actually give this to a new-born baby or to an old person to help strengthen the internal organs and clear the respiratory tract, as well as use it simply to flavour food. I named my business and all my products in her loving memory.

If you came from a well-to-do family in Trinidad then, you were brought up in very strong British traditions; all my teachers were Irish nuns and I learnt Irish and Scottish dancing, we were taught British history and to be obedient to the queen. We had to sing the British national anthem every day and, when I came here, I was amazed that this wasn't practised in British schools and equally amazed that the British children did not know about their own history. When I had my own children and told them this, they felt that my education was a much richer one and they wished they had been taught that way.

My father was an insurance broker who brought us over here to improve our education. We lived in a very upper-middle-class area where my sister and I were the only two black girls in our Essex school. If you came from that sort of background, a British education meant you could go back to the Caribbean with much more prestigious qualifications. My first job here was as a laboratory technician, then I got fed up with that and went to work for a housing association which my father had founded ten years before, at a time when there was a great fight to provide decent housing for the poor. The local authorities were very stagnant in their attitudes and it was a battle to get the local council and the government to provide better homes for people. Coming from a relatively privileged background, I was always aware of the appalling housing conditions in London – I saw real squalor in the East End and I have always been involved in fighting for the underdog.

I deliver a lot of lectures around the country now, particularly to middle-aged women. I tell them that if they have talent, and if they have something to focus on and are prepared to take the risk, they should learn to apply it. The established system has developed in such a way that women, especially working-class women and single parents (who still have a lot of stigma attached to them) need much more than simply ambition if they are to win against male prejudice and the financial institutions which control business. When I was trying to get started in business, I tried to understand the system and tried not to divulge my background at all. I wanted to let them take me at face value. But for a black female single parent, working at face value doesn't work; none of these banks have ever looked at me and my business record and said: 'Well this woman has done a lot on her own.'

It hasn't dawned on them that to get one new product on any supermarket shelf is hard enough, but to get into seven super-markets in two years, which I did, is something unique. It hasn't dawned on them that to establish a new product in a thousand stores nationwide without finance and establish a high profile small business and win national awards is something very special. They still refuse to take me seriously and, even now, I can't even get a £1 overdraft facility.

I started off cooking the product in my own kitchen and fairly soon became aware of the government loan guarantee scheme which I now call, after my experience with it, 'lethal weapon number one' because it provided a false sense of security. In my view it has been one of the most destructive forces for many small businesses who have had the misfortune to use it. It is there for people, like myself, who have no collateral and 70 per cent is secured by the govern-ment. I had to go on income support and even though I started sup-plying Fortnums and Harrods, I couldn't pay myself a wage until I started to supply the supermarkets. You are allowed to borrow up to £100,000 but it took two years of rejection from every single bank before I could get that loan to carry on with the business.

I was lucky because I found a very nice bank manager who was not only a decent man, but was ambitious and courageous and felt my business might help his career – in return for him getting me on the loan guarantee scheme, I had to promote his bank and his branch. The only reason I could see for my rejection until then was that I was out of the norm. At the time I didn't see myself like that, of course. I saw myself as someone who had a great product and wanted to take time to learn the market and get into the mainstream. I didn't think there was anything odd about myself because I was brought up among white, middle-class people in Britain where I did not previously experience any barriers. But suddenly in business I was being judged as a black single parent with all the stereotypical images that accompany that. The idea that I could market in the mainstream, get my product into Harrods, which I did within six months of starting off in my kitchen, seemed incredible to them.

I have never had any negativity from the British people as a whole. The shops and the media were also very receptive; it was the banks and the government authorities. These people who are in control of our lives were the only ones who showed total stubbornness and put up all the barriers I have had to fight. The loan guarantee scheme is poorly maintained, poorly managed, poorly advised and and poorly allocated. Any small business would find it extremely difficult if not altogether impossible to repay a loan of £100,000 in two years at a high interest rate. At the time I didn't realise how much it was going to be, but I needed the money so badly to get out of the kitchen and into a factory that I was forced to continue to live on family credit to maintain my family as every penny the business earned was ploughed back into maintaining the high overheads.

In some ways I'm glad it took five years – even though without those problems, I would have got here at least two years earlier – because money isn't the only thing. You need to make sacrifices and take time to get to know your business well to really make it work. The only training ground you're going to have is the mass of difficulties you face. In a way it is easier for a woman because they have learned to budget and survive on a low income, but you still have to learn the trade and it is down to you to take all the opportunities to make it work. It's a tough game, and you have to be tough to make it, but that doesn't mean you have to emulate or alienate men in any way. I don't believe in all this power dressing. I believe in just being myself, being honest and open and at the same time getting people to realise that, in order to turn a mirage, your dreams, into something solid, a great deal of imagination, determination, sacrifice and hard work is needed. Hard work which is for your benefit and no one else's.

This is the first year I have been on my own, totally self-financed, and we have had our best year because there is no one but the customer controlling us and I am efficient, which is very important. I always have to remember that I am black and the one bad thing that previous black businessmen have left to black women is unreliability, so I have to be aware of my image outside and show that I can be reliable. We have worked twenty-four hours without sleep on occasions to make sure that we get our orders out on time.

It is true that if you are black and want to succeed you have got to have very strong positive attitudes, but that is also true of many white people in this country. Black children are brought up in the same way as white, working-class children and if you compare like with like you would probably find equivalent levels of achievement. Blacks only seem to have more disadvantages because this society harps on them more. I always say to people if I were white and Irish with a strong Irish accent, I would be facing the same barriers. The great thing for me is that I can't change my colour and that is a strong weapon because it gives me a sense of purpose and pride. I have tried to give my two black British daughters a sense of balance, pride and self-worth as well, so much so that my children are both aware of who and what they are and the challenges they are going to meet.

If you have negative parents, you will get negative children. Quite often women, no matter what colour they are, use the fact that they are women as an excuse when they are not fighting for what they want. One of my mottoes is 'a doer is an achiever'; all things in life are possible and mostly people make excuses for why they don't achieve.

Most women are given a completely false image and impression of what it is to become your own boss. I always tell women to take time revaluing themselves. It is great to be afraid, because courage comes out of that, and you learn about your own confidence as you progress and improve. For instance, my greatest achievement has been learning to drive. I was always petrified of driving and I finally learned two years ago, under pressure from my daughters, because I had to do it for my business and I still think it is the most daring thing I ever did. Once I conquered it, I felt great.

One of my other challenges and stepping-stones was walking out on my husband about six years ago, before I started the business. I had known him since I was sixteen but the relationship broke down completely. I know I would never have succeeded with the business if I had stayed with him, because I wouldn't have had the support I needed and which I do have now from my daughters, my mum and dad and the rest of the family. For any mother, or any wife, if you love the man you are with and want to be the perfect mum, perfect wife and perfect housewife, there are just not enough hours in the day to become a successful businesswoman without your partner's total support and understanding.

I used to be a very shy person. When I left my husband I lost all confidence and was on the verge of a nervous breakdown; it took all my strength and my children to build that up again. I used to have a photographic memory but by the time I left there were lots of parts of my life which I just couldn't remember and it has taken me six years to regain a lot of those memories.

Now when I know things are really getting on top of me, which is about every three months, I stay at home, buy a bottle of wine and cry and scream and tear up my emotions completely, but I only let it last twenty-four hours. I call it my 'feel sorry for yourself' day. In this way I use my emotions rather than allow my emotions to use, control or destroy me. I've learned to let it all out instead of keeping it all pent-up like I did in the past. It is extremely therapeutic.

In the past six years I have not only succeeded but also become a new woman; I no longer have to do the family meals because my daughters, who are twenty-two and eighteen, insisted that they were tired of seeing me in the kitchen and wanted to see me cook-ing for pleasure rather than as a chore. I have hardly done any housework for six years either because my younger daughter takes care of the flat and the elder one works fulltime in the business so I can leave it in her charge if necessary. They support me as much as I support them and the nicest thing they have ever said to me was that from birth I was always there for them, so now they want to be here for me.

My elder daughter doesn't want to be a food manufacturer, but she knows what I have been through and has put her career on hold to ensure that I survive, because she knows that if she is never able to get off the ground herself she can fall back on this. They are not highly educated, but they are very intelligent, responsible, sensible and liberated, and even though they have seen what I have been through, they are not put off the idea of running their own busi-nesses because of the example they say I have set them. They know that as long as you are happy within yourself, and know your potential then the world is your oyster. No one should ever be ashamed of who or what they are, or ever deny their background, because it is that which gives each of us a history on which to build.

HILARY ARMSTRONG

'Education is a subject about which I am passionate'

Hilary Armstrong is the Labour MP for Durham North West. She is a former social worker and front-bench spokesperson on education and is now Parliamentary Private Secretary to the Labour leader John Smith.

I was one of three women from the North East who came into the House of Commons in 1987; the other two were Joyce Quinn and Mo Mowlam and we got in more through luck than determination, although we had been very determined from about 1981 onwards when people started saying that there weren't enough women putting themselves forward in the North. Every time there was a seat coming up we made sure one of us was around to stand for selection so they couldn't say we wouldn't do it, but the reality was that you had to keep working away at it. Some of the women's organisations were determined they were going to help. It's a tradition that goes way back to 1927 when the Durham Women's Advisory Council decided they were going to get a woman selected, and in the next by-election and the election after that, they got Marion Phillips, who was then the National Women's Officer, selected for Sunderland and she was elected. There has always been a strong women's organisation in the North East which helped a lot when they decided that they were going to support two or three of us to keep at it.

Because Joyce, who had been the Euro MP, and I had been around for so long, quite a lot of people had stopped seeing us just as women which probably helped a bit. We also really had to demonstrate that in every single area we were reliable, would turn up at every sort of meeting and would do dogsbody work as well. After one selection conference which I failed to win, a woman who has known me since I was a child went up to the fellow who was selected and said: 'Well today has proved that women have not just got to be twice as good as men, they have to be three times as good because Hilary outstripped you all.' I could always count on getting a straight line from the women in the party!

My father, Ernest Armstrong, became a Labour MP the year I left home in the North East to go to college in London. Inevitably your upbringing has a major effect on the way your life develops and the sort of decisions you make, and if you are born into a political family you either go along with it or rebel against it and my dad was such an open, enthusiastic person who never dictated anything that we all got taken along by it. Through most of my childhood he was on the council in Sunderland but my mum was just as important an influence because she worked as a schoolteacher and was determined that she wouldn't be what she called a 'Tory wife' who simply went along to things. So although we were on his first election address when he didn't get elected for Sunderland South in 1959, we weren't on any others.

His main area of activity on the council was education. He was elected chair of the education committee on the platform of taking Sunderland comprehensive so I was caught up in the middle of that; my school was one of the first to be turned comprehensive and I had teachers who were very against it, blaming it all on my dad. My English teacher had me kneeling on a coconut mat while he told the rest of the class that my father was going to be responsible for letting the clot into the cream. Education is still a subject about which I am passionate and if I have one ambition it is to be an education minister in a Labour government. Education is still seen as being for the very bright and we won't get changes until every family sees it as a crucial part of their lives and not just something that you get the kids through until they are sixteen. I know that most individuals are capable of a lot more than they have ever been allowed to develop and that is what is revolutionary about 'real education' and what this government won't allow.

After I moved back up to the North East to work as a social worker, I was chair of the ASTMS regional council for seven years, on the Labour Party regional executive from the union, and was the first woman and the first lay person to be elected in the trade union section. But the unions made it quite clear that I was therefore expendable. I had a massive row one year, about commitment and belief, because one union decided they were going to dump me. It was always necessary to behave in ways which showed them that you weren't going to be used simply when they wanted you.

It is no coincidence that, of the three of us women MPs in the North, none has got kids. The system is simply not geared to women with young children getting into Parliament. The whole party rhetoric, about your commitment to the constituency and accountability to the party, is making it very much more difficult for women. Some of the women MPs who have got young kids and have promised to move to their constituencies are torn apart, not just practically, but by guilt and everything else. I also think that our culture in the North would make it very difficult for me to have a nanny, for example. One of my answers has always been much more devolution of power, because I think the closer the decision-making is to the locality in which women are operating, the better. Women are so effective in community politics. They are always the people who know who's who, in many ways they are already the leaders in their communities without getting the publicly acclaimed positions.

The more you push real decisions down the line, the more women get involved. Being a national politician isn't really a normal job; it isn't a job that is easily sorted out between family responsibilities and Westminster, and we will only make it open for women when men are as involved in the family res-ponsibilities as the women, so that men recognise that Parliament has to be organised to allow you to do the two and that you are a better politician if you have a normal life as well as parliamentary life.

Organising the parliamentary day from nine to five doesn't work because for folk in the North that doesn't make life any easier. We need a shorter week or two weeks on and a week off, or regular blocks of time when you know you are going to be in Westminster, or blocks of time when you know you can be in the constituency so that you can carve out personal time. Sensible politics is about more people who have normal, ordinary day-to-day experience of being involved, so politics has got to be organised in a way which actually celebrates that and doesn't make you frightened to admit to it, which is the case now.

Getting more women involved on a local level is about the way the party organises itself and enables members to take issues up in a way that is real to their own lives and experiences. I have a totally working-class constituency with very few professionals, and their day-to-day experiences mean that we have to organise the party in a way which enables them to feel their life is OK. We are not trying to make them something they are not, or make them feel that the only way they can become involved in the Labour Party is if they stop being working class and enjoying working-class activities. The wine and cheese events don't go down well in North West Durham, but organising in ways which celebrate people's lives and experiences do help women become active.

In my constituency we have a women's section which meets an hour before the branch meeting; the membership is about a hundred in the branch, which is quite good, and about thirty in the women's section. It starts meeting at about 6.30. By the time the men come in, about 7.30, the women are already ensconced, so they are already quite a confident block. It hasn't always been like that though. Before I was selected we did some work around the fact that women had really lost confidence about telling people that they were members of the Labour Party, so we gossiped and it turned out that although it had once been normal for the leaders of the Labour Party in the village to be leaders of the community, by the early 1980s if you were a leader of the community you tried not to let people know you were involved in the Labour Party, and what could we do about this? We got right down to silly things like role play, about how you talk to people about politics so you didn't put them off. We all enjoyed it and through working with them, we worked out what were the things that were most important to people in the village.

Then they actually did some work, going round talking to people and that revolutionised things and enabled them to have confidence in what they are doing so that they could come forward in other ways and recognise their strengths and the positive things they do in their community. I am not saying this is what we should do for people who are confident, who have had an education and who want to be active in a normal way; we should do it for the ordinary women who have had all the negative experiences that our culture has handed out to them in the last thirty years, to give them the confidence to recognise that their daily activity is actually political. I have worked with women who have set up play schemes or who have run campaigns about the school crossing, and they are far better organisers, far better at actually getting things done, at seeing what needs to be done and setting up democratic structures than most men. Then they claim it is not political and the reason for that is that we have marginalised mainstream politics into particular sorts of activity and methods of work. It will not be easy to restructure that, but it can be done.

There are similar problems with the image of feminism. Many women still find 'feminism' very threatening because it threatens the decisions they have made about their lives. They may like to think that, in another world, they would rather things were different, but they are living in this world in a certain way and often they have the sense that feminism undermines the way they are living. Feminism has critically affected my understanding of my life, however. I object to women being told, either by politicians or feminists, that unless they lead their lives in a particular way, then they aren't right on. For me rhetoric has always got to be based on practical day-to-day experience. Theory and practice must interreact so that the decisions that women have made about their own lives, for survival and all sorts of other cultural and social reasons, are valued and built on.

In the Northern region, we have done this very effectively at times. I got the minute book of my local women's section from 1927 to 1932 and most of the minutes are two or three lines and clearly from women who had very little literacy, but they describe, for example, their political education programme over the winter of 1927–28. It involved members of the section being asked to take a session, maybe about work on the Assistance Board, or about about making something. The last session was a questionnaire from one member on what is it that has changed your life as a housewife; they talked about the box mattress instead of the floppy mattress, the needle-threader for the machine, the steam iron, black lacquer for the stove instead of black leading, and then the speaker gave a lecture about 'how we can use this time that has been liberated for us as women, to build socialism'. They were the women who in the early 1980s were described as only ever having made the tea in the Labour Party! Actually what they had done was to understand the daily experiences of their women members and used those for building. They were the women who worked out the organisation of the party and thought about how you canvassed, who you went to see – they had to do it in women's sections because they were miners' wives and if they had gone into the pub, that would have been a scandal and the men wouldn't have stood for it, so they had riotous times on their weekend schools or days away, but they enjoyed a cultural experience which enabled them to build on what they were doing day-by-day and then express that in other ways.

The trick for the party is to let women see that is what we are doing now, to let them see that we are not saying every decision you make, what you wear, what family style you have, your commitment to your kids and whether you work or not, has to be vetted by us. They are decisions that we recognise women will make and we want to support them in that so that they feel they have some choice. When we are talking about giving women opportunities, it is not just giving women opportunities to work or to be a politician, it is just as political to value their cultural experiences and build from those in ways that mean they can be proud of their community and their family and feel that is all right.

One of the problems about being an MP is that it gives you status and most people think you have to live up to the status, rather than recognise that you can only ever do the job with a great army of supporters. I have a branch now in a tiny village, which in 1981 was the poorest village in Durham County, where there are twenty-eight members and three of them are men. The women are the life and soul of my support network in the village (where my dad was born). These women are in and out all the time servicing me and making sure I can do the job – they think it is very important that I go out in clothes that have been ironed – and they are part of my identity in the constituency. Members of Parliament have got to have the confidence to let other people be their face and voice now and then; we have got to be people and not just figureheads and if there were more women MPs it would make an enormous difference in image, in feel, in style. It was an enormous risk for the party leader to have a woman PPS because so much of the job is negotiating with the old guard of the PLP. I hope I have done it in a different way – I can't be the heavy minder.

There is too much pressure in Westminster for women to just become like the men. When I was drafting the party's childcare policy, I got the feeling that some of the men, even though they knew it was important for us to be saying it, never really understood what it meant, but unless childcare becomes part of a general employment and education strategy then it will only ever be an add-on. Even in the Labour Party I think we still have the male breadwinner as the norm and the woman helping out at certain stages in her life and for me all that does is not give women real choice. This concept of full employment, which people still talk about, means seeing the work-force as predominantly male, full-time workers. That is what Keynes meant and Beveridge envisaged and that is what our welfare state was built on, but we now have to look at policy in a totally different way; in terms of women working part-time, but not losing their benefits for example. We talk about universal benefits, yet there are only 15 per cent of women who get their full pension entitlement – it's not a universal benefit for women. The party has enormous opportunities, but the majority of people who are doing the 'thinking' about policy have got to be reminded to think about women's needs at every stage.

DENISE O'DONOGHUE

'Men are happier, with women who make their coffee, not their programmes'

Denise O'Donoghue established Hat Trick Productions, the award-winning television production company, which amongst other programmes, makes Whose Line is it Anyway?, Drop the Dead Donkey *and* Have I got News for You? *She is managing director and chair of the company.*

I am the second eldest of five daughters of parents whose relationship was tempestuous, to say the least. There was a lot of anger and violence in our house and my father was absent a lot of the time. My parents divorced when I was fifteen and we kept up with my father for about a year after that, then I didn't see him for twenty-one years until I found him about seven months before he died of a heart attack.

Ours was very much a female household with no differentiation between what girls and boys might achieve – that was absolutely not a criterion which would determine the boundaries of achievement. My mum was very keen on academic progress and we were all quite bright and had extra coaching, even though we didn't need it, so I did quite well at school. I continued to do quite well after my parents divorced, but didn't take my A levels. Instead I left and worked for four years during the good old days when you could leave school and get a job without having any skills. I was quite good at talking and it wasn't difficult to talk your way into a job.

Then I wanted to be a social worker – the classic solution for a child from a dysfunctional family. Rather than think I had problems of my own, I wanted to look outside and try to sort out other people's. But social work wasn't possible without A levels or a university degree so I did A levels in evening classes and, after about four weeks, decided it wasn't really so difficult and applied for a university place. I then went off to York to read politics, which I absolutely loved.

I chose politics because I was obviously interested in the subject and have always been pro the underdog. I can watch a football match and within thirty seconds be on the side of the teem which is least likely to win! That is the philosophical basis of my own political views. I was also living with someone at the time who was very committed politically and I was very influenced by him; I would never have thought of a political career, though, because I loathe being in the limelight.

I had produced and directed plays at university but after I left I went to work in the City. I enjoyed it in terms of the security it provided, but realised I didn't really fit in. Then the job of director of a trade association of producers came up. I had just split up from my partner of nine years, was deeply miserable and decided to apply for it. The task of writing a CV after splitting up with somebody I'd been with for so long did me a lot of good because it forced me to put down my good points on a bit of paper and I got the job. The organisation was a very influential body which advised and provided information for independent producers about getting programmes commissioned and running a company. At the same time Jimmy Mulville, now my husband, had been involved in two pilot satirical programmes for Thames Television. When they got turned down I had a go at trying to sell them – Channel Four bought them very quickly and I co-produced four series of *Who Dares Wins*.

I suppose it was controversial from the start. In our first programme we did a sketch, which was really about the cynicism of advertising, in which Jesus was on the cross with a background of wonderful ecclesiastical music, then up came the Hamlet cigar advert and Jesus, in his attempt to get the cigar which is being offered to him, fell off the cross. It was demanding and thrilling to produce a show like *Who Dares* because, in the way that sketch shows do, it taught one a great deal about a range of comedy styles. It was while I was doing the series that I thought I could go one step further and set up a company, the aims of which were really to offer writers a chance to be both creatively and financially more involved with their ideas. So Hat Trick was born.

I wouldn't regard myself as the main or even the most important creative inspiration behind Hat Trick – my ability is to enable programmes to be made. The fact is that I think I do have a skill, about which I tend to be a bit cynical and ambivalent, and that is to know where the good ideas are coming from and to know the good people. The editorial policy of Hat Trick is protected by myself and a number of other people who work here and we are just not interested in doing certain types of programmes. There is no doubt that the business side of it is firmly my responsibility, but I don't think I'm anywhere near the best producer I know. Producing is so intense and time-consuming that if I were to do that there would be no time for anything else in terms of developing the company – and we realised very early on that having a positive balance on the balance sheet means that we don't have to make programmes just to pay the rent, which would be the worst outcome of all for me. I could look back on some programmes and say they didn't work out as well as I would have hoped, but I don't look back on any and think: 'Well we had to make that to stay in business, but we were never really keen on it.'

I think it is difficult to characterise Hat Trick; what we are trying to do, and the things we wouldn't do. I don't think our work is really radical or political. I think there is a political dimension in that we share a school of thought and we couldn't do a programme which we felt did not reflect reality or have real people at its heart. We are not, though, a political flagship in the narrow sense. Making funny programmes which make people laugh is the overriding criterion. We are now developing sit-coms for ITV and BBC1 which are not going to be the sort of sit-coms that have been churned out for the last twenty-five years. They are fundamentally rooted in what makes people tick, what motivates them, their fears and their means of surviving in its widest sense. You do not need to caricature to be funny.

It is very difficult for me to put our work into a category, to say what it is that characterises a Hat Trick idea. Of a hundred ideas that might come across my desk, most of them – the vast majority – we wouldn't be interested in. I'm not despairing about what the mass audience watches; my job is not to despair, it is to make the programmes I want to make, and I think there is room for what I want to make. *Whose Line is it Anyway?* spawned a lot of people and they have appeared in other shows. People like Clive Anderson, for example, go back a long way – he used to do the warm-up for *Who Dares Wins* when he was a practising barrister – so there is an extended family of talent, people who enjoy working together.

I think we probably do engender quite a lot of envy which is understandable because television is a very precarious business; there are too many people chasing too few programmes, particularly in the area of documentaries and current affairs. I wasn't aware of prejudice until quite recently because it has only come with the company's success and my identification with the company. In the early days I was an oddity, and an oddity isn't a threat. I think that I have learned to live with the negative side of being a successful woman. If you flutter your eyelids you sell yourself short, if you are businesslike they say you're a hard cow. Personally I'm getting a bit sick of the successful career woman stereotype. I suppose there is an alternative but my perfectionism also means I want to be successful *and* gorgeous. Is that a cop-out? In one article about me and Hat Trick which was unconditionally praising, another unnamed male producer was quoted as saying: 'Yes she is very good, but I don't really like her.' That was the quote they chose to caption the photograph – and it hurt. I don't think I can counter it, you have to get used to it, but it does hurt. I think in the business generally, I am regarded with fear; that isn't just my persona, it's to do with the attitude that men bring to dealing with women in anything other than a subservient world. They are happier with women who make their coffee than make their programmes. I wasn't that much aware of it from the start because I was not some-one who figured in their competition stakes, but the more Hat Trick has done and the more successful we have become, the more I have become aware of their fear.

There is a downside with most men to women's success. I think if you are not prepared to get into a sexual interaction, however unstated, it is very difficult for most men to put you into a category with which they are familiar. The net result is that they don't quite know how to manage the situation. It comes down to a question of control; men like to be in control of women and when there isn't that simple hierarchy in a relationship, it throws them. For men it's like climbing up a mountain with nothing to hold on to, because they have no previous experience of the situation, but rather than say they find the woman difficult to deal with, or they feel threat-ened, or that that they don't understand how the relationship is working because all those sexual stereotypes come in the way, they say: 'It's her fault. It's because she's difficult, tough, unapproach-able,' etc. It is about apportioning blame really.

Whilst I can sit and have this conversation now, I don't have time to take all these things on board when I'm at work and I don't really feel it is my responsibility to. If I am asked a question about someone, I won't make my mind up based on whether or not he meets my expectations, I try to do it on the basis of how good he is at his job. But if you are a woman, that isn't enough. If they throw shit at you, you are not supposed to retaliate because that just plays into their pre-judged ideas about you anyway and if you do retali-ate, then you become a woman who just 'can't take it'. Jimmy and I have an incredibly good relationship now, though it wasn't always the case, and we do work together quite a lot which inevitably pro-duces situations where I am the managing director of the company and here fulltime and he is a director of the company who also has outside commitments. He is incredibly honest about how it affects him as my husband and someone with a financial and emotional interest in the situation.

If you talk to the BBC they will say there are a lot of women coming through in the industry but my experience is that there are still very, very few. There are lot of researchers, secretaries and production managers, but at the end of the day the television industry is no different to any other and the higher you go the fewer women there are.

When I talk about my life like this I suppose it does sound quite easy, and, by my own personal standards of difficulty, it hasn't been that hard. I wouldn't say that as a woman I have to work twice as hard as a man. I do anyway, partly because of growing up in a family with no male, and partly because I am a perfectionist, which is what tends to drive me. My family background meant I definitely identified work as a way of getting out. I have that in common with Jimmy, who is also working class and whose way out was the same as mine – incredibly hard work, over-achievement at school and university. I suppose I have worked hard but it has been my choice.

I have no children of my own, which may have been a sacrifice really. It may still happen – who knows – though the longer it doesn't the more ambivalent I feel about it. My family background meant that having children looked too much like drudgery and exhaustion, because my mum worked all the time and brought us up without any help. Also, because I was the eldest at home – my elder sister was brought up by our grandparents – I helped a lot with the child-rearing. If I had had them earlier I think I would have been hopeless as a mother. It has taken me a long time to process things from my childhood, and I am still doing that. Discovering my father was terribly important to me and important for him too. He was in pretty dire circumstances, but it did help me see him very differently, more compassionately really, and it helped me stop blaming myself for my parents' marriage breakdown. I think children do blame themselves for that – you think that if you had worked harder at school or if you had cleaned the house more, your mum and dad wouldn't be at each other's throats; you become very self-obsessed and desperate to be in control. So I have never regretted finding my dad. At one point I thought: 'My God, what have I done?' but I still went through with it. I have never ever regretted it. It still hurts that it was so short a reconciliation.

BEATRIX CAMPBELL

'There is not one
feminist movement
any more –
there are many'

Beatrix Campbell is a feminist writer and journalist.

Party allegiances are very rugged in Britain. The left has to think very hard about why it is that it can't break that brittle alliance to the Tories, especially amongst women over thirty-five. Women as voters are pessimistic and often don't think that it will make any difference to them which party gets in. They will have had negative experiences of government and of local government, often Labour local government. To be candid, what could you point to, other than the equality legislation, as something the Labour Party has done positively for women? Historically the Labour Party hasn't engaged women as women, even though most feminists have been affiliated to the left. The Tories have been good at speaking to women; what they tell them may be a load of crap, but nonetheless they are engaging them.

Men see any challenge as annihilating. They don't hear women's disappointments. Women make monumental efforts to make relationships with men work. As Dora Russell said: 'They don't co-operate.'

Women have learned to manage their ambitions and disappointments in the political arena. Women, particularly poor women, are accused of being apolitical and apathetic. Often actually they are exhausted, pessimistic and broke. They will have to want change to happen. But they are not interested in going to meetings, watching other people parading, they just haven't got the time. They might be interested if it was going to make a difference, but we are talking about people whose lives are full of heartbreak. They don't want to put themselves into another environment where they might be humiliated or bored.

I feel it myself to a certain extent. I spent most of my twenties and thirties in meetings, rushing. Politics actually was my social life. But it was full of stress and I wouldn't want to do that again, even though I feel the person I am was partly produced by that activity. Women tend not to get involved, just won't get involved in things which aren't useful, simply to enjoy the sport of politics.

There is not one feminist movement any more. There are many. There isn't one women's liberation movement, with an address and a march. The old one clearly came to a point at which it didn't like itself. It was stuck in a way of organising that had been borrowed from the left and from men, with an annual conference and an atmosphere that everybody who was involved in that form of politics in the 1970s will have completely contradictory and ambiguous memories of; loving the disco, loving being at a workshop where you learned things and had access to people who were revelatory, but loathing the plenaries with all the tension and hate and rows that went with passing a single resolution.

So what the women's movement then did was quite brilliant; it abolished itself and 1978 saw the last national women's liberation conference in Britain. By then it was a women's movement with a large constituency, not heterogeneous, full of different sorts of folks with different experiences and different wishes. The things that have survived the women's movement are ideological – intellectual challenge, scholarship and its engagement in popular culture and self-help services that are good and practical like battered women's refuges and rape crisis lines. It exists in informal, useful networks, mostly struggling on very little money, among mothers, workers, survivors.

We may regret the fact that women can't get together and have a march and a sense of belonging to something that can be mobilised at no time. But that is a function of our history. It is a massive problem. Greenham was a very good example of how direct action can have a mighty impact. The miners' strike was another extraordinary moment in politics; here was a strike that was not popular, that was badly organised, that had no strategy, but with goodwill a lot of people organised for a year to keep mining communities in food. The networking that went on probably transgressed political habits and boundaries and was transforming for a lot of the people involved in it.

After the last election two things stuck in my mind. One was the memory of being at a Labour Party conference in the 1980s and hearing Neil Kinnock make a speech which represented a serious contemplative effort to engage with the lives of women, especially about law and order and their entitlement to feel safe. None of that actually appeared in the press reports of the leader's speech. While there was a process of modernisation that confronted the way women had been imagined politically, it went largely uncovered by the national media. Again and again whatever efforts are made to put women onto the political agenda, they don't survive the translation of the political correspondents.

The second realisation was that there isn't anything in most politicians' experience of everyday life – getting a dinner on the table, getting through a day, the organisational skills that women need to mobilise a family – which allows them to relate to most women. Women's needs don't enter the political vocabulary. We have a social services crisis in Britain which is lived daily by millions of exhausted women but which doesn't even touch the debate. There is also a sense that the particular inflexions that women bring to politics are not allowed to define the way that they will be discussed.

GLORIA PULLEN

'My dream is that deaf people will have the same chances as everybody else'

Gloria Pullen is a deaf woman who has done research in the deaf community in Britain and Europe and now works as an adviser for deaf students at Bristol University. She is also on the British Deaf Association's Advocacy Committee which campaigns against discrimination.

The biggest and most serious political issue for us at the moment is education, because that is where good development or problems for deaf children start. Many deaf schools have been closed and many deaf children are in mainstream local schools, where their needs are not met. It is very easy to forget one deaf child in a class of forty children, but giving them equal opportunities at that stage could mean the difference between going to college or university – which at the moment is very difficult – or not. My dream is that one day deaf people will have the same chances as everybody else.

Deaf children often become very isolated. I didn't have that sort of experience myself because I come from a deaf family and I went to a deaf school, but my daughter is deaf and she went to an integrated school and I have learned a lot from her experience of life in the playground, for example, where deaf children are seen as odd. It can also be very isolating for children in a hearing family. One deaf child can be very difficult – he or she can't participate and often parents can't communicate with their deaf child. Then when the child leaves home and moves into the workplace that continues and a pattern is set in childhood which goes on into old age. I got confidence because my family gave it to me and I had role models of what deaf adults could be like, but many deaf children think that when they are fifteen, they are going to die, because they have never met a deaf adult. Bristol University has really concentrated on trying to help hearing parents learn how to help their children, but that is a rare project. We have deaf advisers working with listening families, teaching them signing, so the whole family is involved. They also provide opportunities for parents to share their experiences and talk to deaf adults and workshops for parents with crèches so parents can talk about their experiences.

There is also more hope for deaf parents to foster or adopt children which is important as some children can't get on with their own families and until now they always got sent to hearing families. There are many deaf couples who have always loved the idea of adopting, but in the past they weren't allowed to. The British Deaf Association decided to take that on as a campaign and now there is one deaf couple who have adopted a child and quite a number who foster. For couples who have no children of their own, it really is a dream. The BDA is very tuned into what deaf people themselves want because the chair and the vice chair are both deaf and so all BDA campaigns arise from first-hand experience.

I know there is a debate about whether to teach children to sign. I have a deaf grandson who is two and he can sign really well and he is a very bright boy compared with other deaf children I know with more communication problems, so I think learning to sign is very important and the earlier the better. There is plenty of time to learn speech and hearing later in childhood, but when a child is very young, they should be given as much language as possible. Some children arrive at school and have no language at all. But I think deaf children need a choice. They should be given a choice to speak if they want to, the choice of hearing aids if they want one and the choice to sign. They can always drop it later and go back to speech, but at least you have given the child an option. I had a terrible time at school. I was always being got at because my speech wasn't very good and I relied on signing, but my parents were always there to support me and, as I got to my teenage years, I thought speech was great and I didn't want to sign any more. Then when I got to my first job, which made me really proud, I was broken hearted because no one could understand my speech, which was awful and no one had told me. I sometimes think what would have happened if I had not been supported by my parents and learned to sign. People without the disability argue about it, but deaf people don't argue about what language they use, it is only the professionals who do. People shouldn't be forced to speak if they don't want to. I am happy with the way I am. I don't feel I would be more normal if I spoke, I feel I should be respected in the same way as people with physical disabilities, who wouldn't be expected to walk if they couldn't. What we should have is our needs provided for.

Thanks to people who can sign, there is a deaf culture, but people need to understand that an awful lot more communication and exploiting of potential just isn't happening. I can lip read but it is difficult for me to get my feelings across in speech. It is *really* difficult – like using a foreign language to explain yourself. I want to use my own language and be proud of it, like the Welsh can.

I have had to fight so much discrimination in my life, from the extra I pay in car insurance to exclusion from watching the TV news. Even when there are sub-titles we still don't get the full information – it is always edited down – but surely we have a right to it? I can't go to the cinema at all, or the theatre, although there is some signing occasionally. I face discrimination in every walk of life. Walking to work this morning somebody asked me directions, and I know this area very well, but when I said: 'Slow down, I am deaf', he just apologised and walked off. It was as if I wasn't being allowed to give directions. It felt that because I was deaf he thought I wouldn't know the way even though I was born and brought up in Bristol. The education system doesn't only let people with disabilities down, it fails to teach people who haven't got disabilities how to behave and respect people. I feel like a member of a linguistic minority, because British sign language belongs to a community and, as with children from some ethnic minorities, it is important to learn that language before moving on to literacy in another.

It is also very difficult to find interpreters. There are very few who are fully qualified to the level you would need to interpret for university level work. Some can sign quite well, because they have deaf parents, but they don't have enough linguistic awareness or subject awareness to cope at a professional level. That obviously makes professional life almost impossible for many deaf people. To take teaching, for example, you have to do your teaching practice in an ordinary school, which puts a lot of deaf people off who don't think they can cope with thirty-five hearing pupils. Some deaf people do have very good speech and can control a class but they have struggled against the odds and there are probably no more than a dozen deaf teachers. Yet if they do succeed it sets up a good example for the deaf community and positive role models for deaf children.

This job really came out of the blue because I wasn't an academic – I used to work in a frozen food factory and I was really happy with my job – then someone asked me to come and do a little bit of work in the university and to be honest even the word 'university' terrified me. I was very suspicious about it but when I arrived I got into the project and just learned on the job by talking to people. I still have no qualifications.

The British Deaf Association is always on the look out for more areas of discrimination to campaign against. At the moment the political priority is education because of the closing of schools for the deaf. Those schools are where the deaf culture and the deaf community are. Local education authorities think it will save money and of course there is pressure from other disability groups for integration, which is fine for them because they have a similar language, but we haven't. For many disabilities access to buildings is a big issue, for us it is access to information. Once we get inside the building, how do we learn?

We also need to campaign more on discrimination against deaf women. With the present unemployment deaf women are discriminated against in the job market all the time. If a man, a hearing woman and a deaf woman apply for a job, the deaf woman will be the last to get it. If deaf women are being abused, there are no deaf women's refuges, if there is an emergency or they are in trouble they often can't ring for help or phone the Samaritans, unless they have special equipment. They often have to work in really bad, low-level, unskilled jobs with no opportunities for promotion. If there are courses that may help them get promotion, they either can't get interpreters or the information they need. If they go and see the doctor even, they often can't get an interpreter to go with them and many doctors look down on women and on deaf people so you have two barriers to getting the support you need. More than anything I would like to see some equality in these women's lives.

JACKIE MALTON

'I wanted to do something for society'

Jackie Malton is a Detective Chief Inspector working in west London, where she deals mainly with young offenders. She has been an officer in the Leicestershire Police Force and in the Metropolitan Police flying squad, and was an adviser to the television series Prime Suspect.

I was the youngest of three and I failed the eleven plus. I went to a secondary modern school which I felt wrote us all off in a way and I feel quite angry about it. I can remember having lessons at fourteen about bringing up babies, because that was what they perceived we wanted to do. I was always interested in history, the prisons and the John Howard legal reform, but I was an academic failure and really messed about at school. I went on to college to do A levels but I didn't get any. I wanted to be a probation officer but couldn't because I didn't have the qualifications. I honestly believed in my heart that I wanted to do something for society, so I joined the police. I had no idea what it was going to be like but I thought that way I could fight for the underdog. I felt an underdog myself because I went to a secondary modern school.

When I joined the police in Leicestershire in 1970 there was a separate department for women. We would deal, not very well, with what are now described as 'women's issues'. Women police officers were there purely to deal with searching women, finding missing children, care cases, and looking after babies. I objected strongly because I had joined to be a police officer and had no idea that we would be in this separate department. We were in a different building working seven and a half hours a day, so we never really felt part of the police.

I resented it totally. In the down times they used to put us on the beat and I used to go into an area called the Highfields, which was the red light area, and talk to the prostitutes, which I loved. A lot of the inquiries about missing kids would end up in that area and the older prostitutes never wanted the youngsters to go down the same path so they would guide me to them. I built up a good relationship with the prostitutes and used to go in and have a cup of tea. By chatting, without abusing the relationship, I used to get all sorts of little bits of information and some good crime arrests. When they used to tell me some of the stories about their clients, I had even more respect for them.

It was quite unusual for a woman to get these crime arrests, and a lot of mine were for drugs, and so I went on the drug squad and after three years I passed the exam for sergeant. I was twenty-two, the youngest in the country, and when the Chief Constable said, 'You're a bit too young to be a sergeant,' I replied: 'But you're the youngest Chief Constable in the country,' which he was. I used to get away with absolute cheek.

After the Sex Discrimination Act in 1975, they retained the police women's department but called it the 'Special Inquiry Unit'. It suited some women to do that particular kind of work but if, like me, they didn't want to stay there, they would have to be brought out. They never really wanted a woman officer of sergeant and above to be operational on the streets. When I went into CID as a detective sergeant in plain clothes, women would get all the rubbish, like thefts of prams, and were very much second-rate.

There was one case, involving the theft of a baby by a prostitute, in which I actually got the baby back and found the woman, because of my relationship with her from a few years back. I always treated the prostitutes woman-to-woman, as human beings, but male officers never thought in terms of women having informants and after that they started to take me more seriously. When I took the inspector's exam and became an acting inspector, I was warned by a sympathetic senior officer that they didn't want women operational on the streets, they wanted them in an office, and he advised me to get out. They didn't trust us enough to be out on the streets, the senior women colluded and there is still a residue of that. I went on a hostage negotiators course when I joined the Met and I was told by an officer from another force that they would not use women negotiators for women terrorists because it was patronising to the terrorist. The Metropolitan Police would never say that, but that is not the case everywhere.

I was one woman in forty when I joined the flying squad in Rotherhithe in south-east London. They introduced me to my partner who was six foot something and he said to me: '•••• off – I'm not working with a woman.' I worked with him for six months before I couldn't stand it any longer and had to swop partners. That was where I got the nickname 'the tart' which was later incorporated into *Prime Suspect*.

I wouldn't say it was a hostile environment, but it takes a certain sort of personality to deal with it and I was 'gobby' enough to handle it. I wouldn't take any stick. In those circumstances, you have got to be good at your job and tough enough to stick up for yourself, otherwise you would just cry. In those days I could not have sued for sexual harassment but today, given the same situation, I would because we need to put it on the agenda. They knew that I was a provincial officer, so they used to treat me as a country bumpkin and say things like: 'Ever given evidence down the Old Bailey, tart?' and then they would mark me in the witness box, for presentation and so on. The only way to deal with it was to laugh at it – if you didn't you would be so hurt and who would you complain to? But I learned so much there and got tremendous amounts of confidence, working at the Old Bailey with the top defence lawyers – some of whom were brilliant at destroying police credibility.

Some senior women officers collude with that system because they are looking for the next rank. It takes a very strong kind of woman, like Alison Halford, to say: 'Hold on, let's just re-examine this,' as opposed to making senior police officers feel very comfortable, which you can do as a woman if you continually agree with them and boost their own prejudices and egos. If you question things, that can affront them. I have been described as too powerful and told that I frighten men. My reaction is: 'Whose problem is that?' but they still put the onus on me.

After the Alison Halford case finished, a number of senior women police officers were interviewed in the media, the majority of whom said they didn't think Alison Halford had done the police service any good at all. That was the easiest thing to say, but I think it is sad. A lot of senior women might find what I say very upsetting but I do think it takes a particular strength of character to speak out. If you researched the number of women who publicly spoke for Alison Halford you would probably only find me. I believe it took strength of character to do what she did. As far as I am concerned she was ahead of her game. If she walked into a room now you would know it because she is funny, articulate, charming and has no fear, and that is what I admire. If that had been me I would have thrown the towel in. Emotionally I couldn't have coped with it. They went on about her drinking and used all the old stereotypes, like it being all right for men to drink but not for women. I think some of those stereotypes are fading away. Nowadays there is a different breed of officer who has been brought up looking at equal opportunities; legislation has taught them to be far more aware of what they can and can't say and there are more young women and men coming in who won't stand for it. There is a feeling that if we don't treat each other right, how do you go out and treat the public right? We are looking at quality of service, at leadership, about how we respond to the public and each other, because there is a huge support system of civilians and until now it was always them and us and the civilians often felt second-rate. It is about respecting each other.

The law is also making progress in the way it treats women. There are only a handful of divisions that don't have domestic violence units now. I sit on a working party looking at the definition of domestic violence and training. We have gone down the line of multi-agency approach to domestic violence and we now support and empower women. In Hammersmith, we have actually set up a drop-in for women in a non-police building to give them assertiveness training. We have got domestic violence intervention projects to address the male offenders. In fact, the police have probably done more than any other agency about domestic violence. Now what we have to do is educate the criminal justice system about the seriousness of it. The tape made by the girl in the Ealing vicarage rape, and the value judgements that were made about the effect it had on her because she didn't show any external wounds, is now part of the training for judges.

Sir Peter Imbert, when he was Chief Constable of the Thames Valley, very bravely allowed that programme called *Fly on the wall* to go out. It showed officers investigating a rape and that was a turning point as far as the police were concerned. In my time we were told to initially disbelieve the victim in a rape case, the excuse being that she would get that line of questioning in a court. Now they are taught to believe her automatically and you assume that she is telling you the truth.

We still have a problem trying to reach the women in the Asian community because it is generally part of the culture that any problems are kept within the family. There are organisations such as Southall Black Sisters and if it weren't for them there wouldn't be anyone else. It is about bridge building and I hope we are making some progress with that because there are some organisations, like Rape Crisis and Women's Aid, with whom we had no relationship at all five years ago and now they talk to us.

Most of my friends are out of the police force. I think there is a terrible danger that if you are associated with the police, and that is all your social life consists of, then you are going to have a very very narrow view of life. I want to keep educating myself and listen to other people's perspectives and points of view.

Peter Guy

BRENDA CROSBY

*'Caring is very lonely –
you are invisible'*

Brenda Crosby, one of the country's six million or more carers, looks after her husband Cec, a stroke victim, on the Flyde Peninsula near Blackpool.

None of us knew anything about caring when Cec had his stroke five years ago. One day I was a company director's wife, respected in the community, with quite a pleasant life, and the next day I was invisible. As it has turned out, we have more friends than we ever had before, real friends, but at first so-called friends deserted us and we don't even see two of our children any more because they couldn't cope with it. Lots of people just walk away from it. I have analysed it as the fear that it could happen to them and they don't want to know it could happen to them – you have to face up to your own mortality when something like that happens.

At first it was very personal and I couldn't speak to anyone without breaking down in tears – I used to do it in front of workmen and anyone who came into the house. That went on for about twelve months, but then I got angry because of the things that I had to go through. I got so angry that I used that anger to do something about the situation.

Cec had his stroke on July 23 1987. He was fifty-eight and, from what we know now, we can pinpoint the times when he had minor strokes before, but at the time it came right out of the blue. It was a very bad stroke and we didn't think he was going to come through it, then they told me he would never walk again and would be a virtual vegetable. When we brought him home from the hospital, he was incontinent and didn't know what was going on, I was in the utmost pain from lifting him in the hospital and we hadn't even got a commode – a friendly nurse had to lend me one. We had no social services so I called a doctor who gave me a prescription for Panadol, which created another problem because I had to get to the chemist to get it. I ended up the next day in casualty and got a collar round my neck for my back pain and I was OK then, but nobody gave us any information.

Before he had the stroke I knew there was something wrong with him. I was going to the doctor myself with vague abdominal pains, which we afterwards learned meant I needed surgery, and I used to get upset because the doctor wouldn't listen to me when I said he was ill – I was obviously to her the typical menopausal woman and was given tranquillisers. Then when the catastrophe happened it was an 'I told you so situation' which wasn't very satisfying, so of course I felt resentment. He was ill and I felt that if they had done something the stroke wouldn't have happened. A carers' survey showed that two out of every three carers suffer from some sort of medical problem directly related to their caring role, either from the carrying or the stress.

My own daddy died in the 1930s when I was four. He was on the dole and didn't get medical attention. My mother died when I was eleven so all through my teenage years I was looking after my step-father who wouldn't let me stay on at school because he thought women ought to get married. I got married when I was twenty, brought up my children, went back and did A levels, went to university, got my BA and then my Masters degree, then Cec had his stroke and I was back in the same position that I had been when I was twelve years old, so I was very angry about all that. I had signed up for a teacher training course a few weeks before he had his stroke and I bribed and cajoled people to look after him while I did it. I am jolly glad that I did now because it has given me an outlet.

*

The Carers National Association came into existence around that time out of what had been two smaller associations. I must have seen the association advertised somewhere, so I became a member. I didn't really expect anything of them – I just thought: 'Well, I am a carer and this is like a union.' For about six months I tried to start an association here but nobody was interested, then there was an article in the local paper about three women who were caring, which said if anyone was interested, to contact them, so I rang them up and we had a meeting here and decided to form a group and it has gone from there. We now have 220 members just in the Fylde. There are quite a number of men – 40 per cent of carers nationally are men – and at our meetings, which I understand are better attended than anywhere else in the country, we regularly get about three or four men out of thirty. We have speakers and I use my teaching skills to get people to do things.

Every so often we have a free meeting and all the members do a sort of mini-biography because that helps the new ones and people learn from each other. We have all become friends, very close friends, and very often friendships are formed between two or three people who get a sitter before a committee meeting, have lunch and come along. We have a helpline with the help of British Telecom, who gave us £250, which anyone can phone up. We believe there are 42,000 carers in the area and think there are six to seven million nationwide and they don't all care for the elderly; 50 per cent care for husbands, wives or children.

Our meetings give people the opportunity to express how they are feeling and the opportunity not to have to pretend that everything is rosy and that they are coping. People get the opportunity to off-load a lot of the frustration and anger which tends to build up at the beginning, when it is a matter of pride that you are coping with your life and it is very difficult to admit that things are getting out of control.

I lecture at Victoria Hospital to nurses and I always say to them that there are several areas in which people need help. They need financial and technological help and shared care in the form of respite care and the opportunity to have a break. Then there is training, education and assessment, which was practically non-existent when we started, and emotional support and information which is what we give on our helpline.

I don't aim to give counselling because I haven't been trained for it, but very often I just listen to somebody cry at the other end of the line. Caring is very lonely. You feel very isolated because you are invisible and lots of people whom you once considered were friends don't want to know you any more. Lots of people are dealing with Alzheimer's patients who don't even know their loved ones, lots of them say to me that they are caring for a husband or wife who doesn't know them and if they get aggressive, they lash out at the nearest person. It is particularly lonely on bank holidays and weekends, when there are no social services and nobody you can call on in a crisis. I always say that from Friday at five o'clock to Monday at nine o'clock I am social services in this area, because you have to phone Blackburn to get anybody and they are not going to come out unless it is an emergency.

Of course we also need more money. It costs a lot more money to run a household when you are caring. We are saving the state money because we want to care for our relatives at home. A lot of my members say: 'If I put him into care, they will pay £280 a week for him, but they won't give me anything.' They offered me invalid care allowance but I refused it because they took a similar amount of my husband's invalidity benefit and his invalidity benefit is untaxed. People have terrible problems trying to hold down a job when they are caring, but sometimes they have to. I get paid for the lectures at the hospital and they offer me £17 an hour, but I can only take £11.50, otherwise my husband's benefit suffers.

If you are in a well-paid job, sometimes it is worth sticking with it, not taking the benefit and paying for everything out of your own income, but then you have to pay for everything out of taxed income. We do have a lot of people with part-time jobs and it may be that they don't make a lot out of it financially, but it gets them out of the house, which if they stayed in could take them to screaming pitch.

You can see my husband now, sitting there looking perfectly

normal, tidy and lucid, and mostly he is that way, but he had brain damage and he can become violent and extremely abusive and that usually happens when we are in a stressful situation. When I was Carer of the Year, we won a weekend away and because he was under stress when I was booking into the hotel, trying to bring in all the luggage, he was shouting and swearing and calling me a stupid woman. That is what takes you to screaming pitch; you feel then that nothing will bring a response because he is totally illogical, then afterwards he says he is sorry.

I call it a mini-bereavement. You have lost that person you married and that person with whom you used to share the responsibility and the chores. It worries me sick maintaining this house because he was constantly doing that sort of thing before he became ill. But instead of a normal bereavement, you have a totally dependent person that you have to look after, so you can't grieve like a normal widow could grieve and then go out and start a new life. Lots of the men in our group are only in their forties and they sometimes solve this problem by having a girlfriend. They still love their wives, but they couldn't get through otherwise.

Some people don't stick it, they just put the other person into fulltime care or walk away from the problems, like two of my daughters have done. That is very hurtful, especially as one of them has my grandchildren and I haven't seen them for four years. But you have to live with life as it is. They stayed with the situation for about twelve months and then, when I had to have major surgery and was at my wits' end and nobody had told me there was respite care, the two girls went. I think they feared they were going to be landed with both of us. That was a very lonely time because I wasn't able to do very much and I wasn't able to manage, but our third daughter is great, she comes up regularly.

Not every region has a network as good as ours, and my heart sinks when I hear about public spending cuts because I know there is no room for more cuts and then I find it very difficult to be positive about anything. Forty per cent of carers are male and I have to constantly tell myself that it is not a feminist issue, while my gut feeling is telling me all the time that it is, because in a sense the men become honorary women; they are trapped in the home and the feminine caring instincts come to the fore. It can be horrific for them too; I see men, macho men, who are watching their wives waste away before them, with small children to support and who admit it is very hard for them to cry. It is a sisterhood, but we mustn't forget those 40 per cent of men, a lot of whom are aged seventy-five and over. It is very heart-rending to get an eighty-five-year-old man crying at the other end of the phone.

I have never been a socialist. I was a liberal who read philosophy at university and fell in love with John Stuart Mill and sort of worked on that basis. I was never active politically or a member of a party, but I was always radical. If I was told I had to join a political party now I would certainly join the Labour Party. After the general election I spent about two weeks in the depths of despair, not really seeing how we could come out of it, and then I felt I had to do something positive like shouting very loudly and hoping someone would give us more hope.

Most people in society want to put carers and caring to the back of their minds because it reminds them of their own mortality. I think we should become more punchy and maybe more shocking in our campaigning, but then there's the danger that people will just say, 'It's that awful Lancashire political woman,' and not really listen. It may be that there are too many middle-class people in control, but if you are in a caring situation you are not going to stay middle class very long.

It has got to start at the top. We have got to have a caring government and better services and recognition that carers are doing a valuable job that is saving the country money. There should be more of a balance between what the government will pay for care to someone who has really got their back to the wall and what they could pay to someone who does it really well and lovingly and gets nothing for it. I don't feel that the younger generation will put up with what our age group puts up with, they won't give up their jobs and take responsibility for two lives. I know you do it when you have got children, but you know what is going to happen, you know how long your sentence is and you know that the outcome is going to be pleasant. All carers have to look forward to, in terms of relief, is the death of a loved one.

Because of the drive the government now has for through-put, to get people out of hospital, patients sometimes come out not wholly recovered, needing dressings and that sort of thing. That puts an extra load on district nurses. If you are disabled and sick, you are at the bottom of the list, but if you are disabled, sick and with a carer, you have just got to get on with it. The GPs are the gate-keepers and they don't seem to want to get involved in the social services side of it. I think they are frightened that if they explained everything that is available the system wouldn't cope. If every one of the six million carers demanded their rights the state would collapse. Somebody said we should all go on strike but I said, 'Who would know?'

We have lots of people who are widows or widowers who ring me up and want to talk and I find it very difficult to cope with because they are so lonely; they want to talk for a long time and I feel it is not quite my remit, yet who do I put them on to? If it is a very bad case I call in social services.

My husband's consultant and I have agreed over a period of time that I could leave Cec for one, then two and now five hours and we have a very good neighbour who is a doctor and whose wife is a nursing sister and she will look in on him. In some ways my activity has been the making of him. He has gone from being a virtual vegetable to having a life of his own. He has become a human being again. What I have done has brought him out of this depression. He says he feels like Prince Philip because everywhere he goes, they know me and he gets the reflected glory. I am known now by some of the professional bodies who treat me like a professional. I am chairperson of Carers National Fylde Coast Branch, and on the national committee.

Sometimes I want out, like when I come back from being away and he has had respite care. Respite care causes problems in itself because you suffer guilt for the first week about leaving them, then by the beginning of the second week you start dreading them coming back, so it is a mish-mash of emotions. Even so I don't really want it any other way. I never say I wish it was like it was. I don't want it like it was. I do not want to sound egotistical here because a lot of people have helped me – but I do feel I have achieved something.

JULIET STEVENSON

'Women are rarely allowed to be ugly, furious, outrageous on stage'

Juliet Stevenson is an actress whose recent work has included the award-winning film Truly Madly Deeply *and a highly acclaimed performance in the stage play* Death and the Maiden *in which she played a torture victim.*

I think I am quite 'tunnel-visioned' about the work I do. When something is starting off in my head, I do become obsessed but I think that is necessary to a certain extent to cope with this weird way of life. I am an army daughter. My father was a brigadier and, for a while, I thought that itinerant early life must have affected my ability to make relationships. If every relationship you make from the time you are born until your adolescence is by definition a finite one, because after two years you are going to be uprooted so that you can't even phone your old mates, then it must have an effect on your conception of what forming relationships is about. Most of the close friends I have now, I have had for many, many years. So it is not as simple as saying every two years I throw out my address book and start a new one. But throughout my twenties, I was very restless and loved the fact that this job meant that every time I moved on, I made a new home – not in a literal sense, but in the sense of creating a new community, whether it is around the making of a play or a film. I love the transitoriness of it in a way, although now I am in my thirties

I have more of an instinct to seek for the permanent and want to put down roots for the first time.

I went to army school overseas first and then to a boarding school over here. It was very progressive and, in retrospect, I must have loved the continuity. They decided to send me over here because I was not managing very well with the army education which is very erratic. Sometimes the level of teaching was very poor, and I can remember being aged eight in a class of forty, where the oldest child was fifteen, and I know I didn't learn anything there.

Where did my politics start? Children always say things are not fair, and in a sense they are natural egalitarians because they demand to be treated as people in their own right who can choose. I remember feeling that when I was about five or six and what I believe now is an evolution of that. I can remember living in Malta and driving around the suburbs of the towns, where conditions were incredibly bad and where people were living in poverty. I became very conscious of my privileged life. Of course the army is very hierarchical and I remember not being able to make sense of why one set of people had one lifestyle and another set had a different one. I would never be a success as a politician though. One thing I have discovered is that I am hopeless in situations like committees. I also don't know whether temperamentally I could cope with the single-minded objective and putting up with so much nonsense thrown at me as a public figure.

When I was at the RSC my politics came out in terms of trying, with others, to get the company to redress the balance in how many women were employed there. When I first joined, all of the twelve associate directors were men, which struck me as odd. Then I got more involved in the Shakespeare plays, which are so often concerned with gender. So many of the plays involve women dressing up as men, because it is the only way they can explore themselves or discover who they really are. Issues of gender and the relationships between men and women are absolutely central questions which are explored in great depth and complexity all the time. I began to feel very strongly not that women would qualitatively be any better, but that it would be interesting if, from time to time, the plays were interpreted from a female perspective, if there is such a thing. The RSC never punished any of us for being stroppy about this and they did respond in the end and there are now more women there. I still worry that it could change at any time and that it could become unfashionable for women to be given an equal chance. As we all know, when things get tough economically, women are often the first to suffer and in recession, people become more conservative. So we have to be vigilant and make sure things don't slide back to the way they were.

I am dying to do Cleopatra. Being old enough to play her will be the one compensation for arriving at middle age. She is so idio-syncratic and doesn't exist in the play to serve anyone else. I have never had any great desire to play all the girlfriends – the Ophelias or Desdemonas and those poor creatures who pad around having terrible things done to them.

It is hard to tear yourself away from a good part, but it often feeds you back as much energy as you give out. We did *Death and the Maiden* for nearly a year in the end and it went on feeding me so much that I found it terribly hard to let go. I went to Prague the day after I finished doing it and heard a clock in one of the old town squares chime nine o'clock, which was eight o'clock in England, and I suddenly realised that the show was going up without me and I couldn't believe it. I felt like a mother who has given her child away to foster parents and can't believe that the child could get through a day without her.

It has taken a long time to let go because the play was about so much more than one individual, it was about a whole world of experience which I was incredibly lucky and privileged to explore and tell. It coincided with the Gulf War, during which I found myself repeatedly wondering how do people whose lives are being brutalised on a daily basis cope; how do women who have seen their husbands mutilated in the morning get their kids fed and washed? So the play felt very timely because it was exploring those things and going behind the news and exploring the human situation. You could feel the response of the audience, and the energy from them gave me an immediate charge. I don't think audiences are ever really aware of how much they contribute and I don't think an evening went by when I didn't relish it. It was a wonderful part because I could take it in any direction. Women are very rarely allowed to be ugly, furious, outrageous and manipulative on stage. They are usually squeezing themselves into some shape which is much more two-dimensional. It was the part of a lifetime. I loved waking up every day knowing that what I did had a value in the community in which we work. I don't feel that about everything we do, even some Shakespeare, and the nature of the audiences we play to. I don't want to play exclusively to audiences who can afford to pay at least £20 a seat.

I wasn't sure about whether I really had the right to play that role but I did talk to people who had had similar experiences. I read a lot of Latin American literature and sought out quite a few members of the Chilean community here who were very generous, and we made links with the Medical Foundation for Torture Victims, which deals with these experiences daily. I spent a lot of early mornings and late nights seeking out people who had lived through those experiences, or who had dealt with people who had.

What I love about being an actor is that you can use almost anything that happens to you and channel it. It is like recycling glass. I am shameless about that. If I had a child I might not use that relationship in my work because I think the only time to be very careful is when you are using aspects of your life in your work which might reflect back on your life. Usually it is very cathartic though, almost like therapy, and nothing is wasted. On *Truly Madly Deeply* I carted my diaries around and shoved them under bits of the set and dipped into them to try and keep things fresh and plug back into other experiences. I do jot things down thoughts or people I meet – partly for that reason, so I can tap back into them.

I tend to live for now, and don't see many certainties in the future. I think I am a bit panicked by certainties. What panics me is knowing what I will be doing in a year's time. I feel much safer not knowing and I think the world is divided into people who need the certainty of planning and others who need the certainty of not. I am definitely the latter, but there are some things, like having a child, that I would like. I have never had a game plan in my head though. I just look around at what is available and make choices and pursue those quite relentlessly, which in itself is a privilege.

MARGARET MEEK

'Now, as never before, reading and writing are about power'

Margaret Meek is a teacher of English, a critic and reviewer of books for children. In 1970 she was awarded the Eleanor Farjeon Prize for services to children and literature. She is now Reader Emeritus of the Institute of Education in the University of London where she taught for twenty three years. Her books are Learning to Read, How Texts Teach What Readers Learn *and* On Being Literate.

As a child I was chronically asthmatic, so that running about in the east winds of Fife winters brought on fearsome attacks. Confinement indoors meant that I had time to read, without interruption, whatever I could find around me: *The People's Friend*, newspapers, the church magazine, novels by Scott, Stevenson and Dickens, local tales, my mother's Sunday school prizes, lots of poetry, especially ballads, which my grandmother taught me to recite to show off. I scarcely remember any children's books, except for some puffboard annuals, which is probably why I fell on them with such delight later. Pooh, the characters in *The Wind in the Willows*, and Peter Rabbit were in strange English books. Tam o'Shanter was more familiar. There was a vague worry when I was unwell that my mind was overheated with too much reading, but no one ever tried to stop me.

My mother speaks very little about her youth. There is a picture in an old album of her in a group of women with a banner, probably suffragettes of the later period, about 1918, when she was a student. I did once overhear her telling my father that she did not think it right to favour boys in families at the expense of the girls. I know I was nine at the time and not aware of the significance of the remark, but she encouraged every initiative of my childhood and adolescence, although I was given to feeling sorry for myself and complaining. My father was a musician by inclination and an engineer by profession. He joined the family business, then, during the war, worked in the naval dockyard at Rosyth. He had nine brothers who formed a choir and sang solos at soirées. In the house of my paternal grandparents there was always someone practising *Rest in the Lord* or *O ruddier than the cherry* just before I fell asleep. I went to the kirk with my maternal grandparents, listened to long sermons and read the story of Ruth or Samuel, hoping that their calling would never be mine. My childhood seems to have been full of the wireless, news items about what we feared was to come, and comic programmes to delay the terror. I specially liked Evensong from English cathedrals, the flutey boys' voices singing the pointed prose of the Psalms, so much less militant than the Scottish metrical versions, although these had a sureness I found comforting.

When I was twelve my family moved to Dunfermline, the home of the fifteenth-century poet, Henryson, the resting place of Robert the Bruce and the birthplace of Andrew Carnegie, bene-factor of libraries, Scottish students and other good works as the result of entrepreneurial success in the steel mills of Pittsburgh. The Carnegie library was at the end of our street. I remember it as a very grand building, with portals rather than doors, although nowadays it seems scruffy with posters and pamphlets. In my schooldays it was a place for serious reading. The children's library upstairs was a revelation. I had no idea that there were so many books for people of my age which I could read fast, whole series of stories about a chalet school. Although borrowers were allowed to take out only one book a day, the librarian let me change mine in the afternoon if I'd finished it, so that I could have another for the evenings and bedtime.

After two years of making myself at home in the building, I

moved into the lofty reference room, with its distant ceiling, tall
bookcases with huge dictionaries and atlases and a special Burns
archive. During blacked-out evenings I sat at a fine oak desk with
a bookrest and a lamp, doing my homework: Latin, French, maths,
the essays of Addison and Steele. Later there came Chaucer's
Prologue. There was always Shakespeare – a different play every
term, and something to learn by heart. I watched the older boys
from my high school, casual, yet self-conscious, looking at the illus-
trations in a big edition of *The Decameron*. Not quite sure what the
attraction was, I read it after they had gone, and found wonderful
tales I knew I shouldn't boast about. In the reading room on the
ground floor I discovered more newspapers than the *Scotsman* and
the *Dundee Courier*, so I chose the *Illustrated London News* where I
saw pictures of the blitz and a notice of Virginia Woolf's suicide.
My teachers spoke of the *New Statesman*, which I didn't always
understand, although I liked the competitions. I entered one which
asked for an interesting parenthesis. I'd found a good example in a
book I was reading called *Sweet Thames Run Softly*. It is still the
only competition I've ever won.

Don't think all this is the exceptional reading of a precociously
bookish child and a tiresome adolescent. It was mostly curiosity
about a world which was full of violent action elsewhere and a long-
ing, often, to be elsewhere, of the kind that the young now satisfy
with television. 'Swotting', the fairly relentless plod through an
unremitting school curriculum designed for boys, was what school
offered. If I enjoyed a lot of it, this was the result of the support of
my studious grandfather who relieved the endless memorising with
a different kind of memoriousness. I trailed after him round book-
shops as he looked for second-hand books with black gothic script
and volumes of sermons. It was simply taken for granted that we'd
go to university, so the exams came and went. I read philosophy
and English at Edinburgh as an undergraduate in the company of
distinguished scholars whose retirement had been interrupted by
the war. I learned to sing madrigals and persisted in the kind of
study that my friend Jane Miller calls 'learned androgyny'. I tried
to outface the prospect of having to be a teacher, now that I knew

that the diplomatic service had no place for women ambassadors, but alternative employment, such as reading books for money, seemed unlikely.

Good friends encouraged me to come to London to see if my asthma and my curved spine could be sorted out. I accepted a job in a rather grand finishing school for girls in Hertfordshire from which I could go to St Thomas's twice a week. Alongside my pupils, clever girls who had spent the war years in glamorous parts of the Commonwealth, I learned to curtsy and to take off my coat in the opera without disturbing my neighbour. As the pupils were not much younger than I was they might have complained about my inexperience. Instead they tolerated it and taught each other in small tutorial groups, sailed into grand English and French universities, or married ambassadors. Then I too went to France and began the love affair with that land, language and culture which has lasted ever since. There I discovered teaching as the life of the mind and never afterwards wanted to repudiate the idea of being an intellectual. Instead that was the badge of belonging I had longed for. So, poorer than a church mouse, I went back to London to earn the right to teach. In the Senate House of the university I found good cheap food, and another splendid library.

About thirty years ago two French scholars, Marie and Jacques Ozouf, made a national survey of French schoolteachers still alive who had taught between 1871, the beginning of compulsory school attendance, and 1914, the beginning of the next period of great social change. These studies produced a revelatory picture of a whole society. I've often wondered if the recollections of those who, like me, began to teach in the schools of England just after the implementations of the 1945 Education Act, would reveal the general sense of optimism I clearly remember and always associate with that time. My impression is that teachers really did believe that education could remove some of the inequalities of social life, and even solve some of the world's problems. In the minds of other people this recollection contributes to their belief that reading was better taught in the past. However optimistic I was,

I can be certain that I knew this was never the case. In my teaching practice school in Brondesbury I taught children who had had very little reading practice in their primary schools, and in other places I encountered adults who had, as yet, no television to give them a window on the world it later came to transform. In both the children and their non-reading elders, the view of the task that stood in the way of their successful learning was their conviction that literacy was not for 'people like us'. By teaching them to read I hoped I was persuading them that they did not have to believe all that they read in a newspaper. Reading was also a way of fighting back against the ideas of others who dominated their lives. I hope we may one day have more knowledge of this period.

At one point in the early fifties a number of things seemed to come together for me, events that shaped my more radical convictions about reading and its relation to the wider aspects of literacy. I was now in a girls' grammar school, full of confident teachers who clutched to their bosoms their particular expertise and their pupils' exercise books as they shut themselves behind the closed doors of their classrooms. Worriedly wondering if I could ask my head of department about the dreadful book from which I was expected to teach the art of précis, a notable lacuna in my early experience, I saw a notice on the board. A new London Association for the Teaching of English (LATE) was about to be formed. So I could go there and ask about précis without loss of face. In fact, after the first meeting, my life changed. Here were truly radical teachers who looked at *learning*. Those who know James Britton, Nancy Martin and Harold Rosen understand what I mean. I was caught up into the research into comprehension, the secondary school word for the interpretation of texts presented in examinations. I found myself in a different professional milieu, one where experience could be analysed and theorised by means of the shared exemplars of classroom practice.

Long ago as that now seems, I discovered then that teachers have to work both with and against the assessments embodied in the national examination systems. With, because their obligation is to see that their pupils are given full value in the ways that the world reads value into numbers; against, when the nature or the procedures of the examination do not let the pupils display what they know best. Given my own experience as a pupil I might have said: 'Just get your head down and learn it' to any pupil who queried texts or pedagogies in comprehension lessons. Now, in LATE, we were trying to make the questions on a piece of text read in an examination reflect what we understood of the reading process itself. We began by inspecting what we did when *we* read and found, of course, a whole range of styles, all of which could be counted as individually successful, but when put together, gave a richer, more satisfactory rendering of what the text contained. It sounds easy; it is, in fact, now as then, very complex. And it is the very complexity of reading as a generative language act that poses problems for examiners, while it is the very stuff of teaching anyone to read at any stage or level of education.

The result of the LATE investigations, demonstrations and persistence was a change in the kind of examination paper later set for O level English language, the one that used to confer the accolade of literacy on most school leavers. From that experience I emerged with an unshakeable conviction that all children get better at reading by reading more whole texts, those that let them know reading as a complete act, something that matters. It even makes them better at précis.

All of this was buzzing in my head when I went to Salzburg to read American literature with Alfred Kazin and American history with Henry Commager. In the castle that later featured in *The Sound of Music* was a great gathering of students and researchers whose friendships were cemented before the Iron Curtain came down and the Berlin Wall went up. It was a glimpse of what Europe could be like. Back in London I continued to teach so-called 'illiterates' and then went to Leeds to do more comprehension research and to teach boys in a school where no woman had ever taught before. We read *Mansfield Park* together, and I discovered how differently the boys regarded Fanny Price from my expectations of them. By this time I had discovered the 'remedial' class and individual lessons for pupils to be in need of 'treatment'. Here the teacher, armed with the latest 'diagnostic' tools (i.e. tests), gave pupils more of what they couldn't do, or little bits of word work to build into sentences. Then six months in the United States, looking at 'reading clinics' in most of the principal cities and at Harvard University, persuaded me that the emphasis on children's failure was far outstripping our understanding of their success. The 'specialists' seemed to be missing the point. When we spoke about reading, very few were interested in the nature of texts or took any account of what, for example, writers said about reading. It took me a long time to realise that I was up against the powerful dominance of behaviourism in the theory and practice of reading. I knew little of the work of training colleges where reading was not a matter for the department of English studies but a domain of educational psychology. The competing definitions and methodologies of this division are still those that beleaguered discussions of teaching reading nearly forty years later.

So, I began again; this time to look at every single method and 'approach' used in schools, impelled by the acknowledgement that many teachers pin their faith on 'schemes' to demonstrate children's reading progress, especially in classes with more than thirty pupils. I tried 'remediation' for a time, with little conviction. The exercises seemed to me to do great injustice to the real nature of the English language, and to present a view of the task which I found unhelpful. The boys in Bristol who came to the club which Denis Stott founded for unclubbable illiterates included the twin sons of a convicted murderer and youths with Down's syndrome. They were moved to read not by the word games we played but by their great pleasure in being read to, the assurance that they would succeed, and the explanations of what they wanted to know about the words on the page. Evidence of this kind rarely saw the light in journals which carried hundreds of articles about reading failure and never one about success initiated by the learners. When, in the sixties, I was at home with my own children, editing the reviews section of *The School Librarian* (I saw most children's books over a period of twenty-five years), I realised it was time to firm up my experience and understanding into interrogation and debate.

Three things stood out. Most reading experts saw reading as different acts of perception: looking at letters or words as shapes or correspondences. The process of reading was called 'decoding'. I saw the power of reading in stories; the fluent move of meaning in the 'primary act of mind'. Teachers were taught reading as a closed system of rules. I saw it as a way of dealing with the social acts of literacy in a society which needed people to be capable of devising and responding to 'all kinds of writing'. Specialists said that there were reading 'levels': beginnings, intermediate and higher-level 'skills'. I saw language as recursive, layered, responsive to purposes, and complex, as literature is complex. Researchers devised experiments; I read literary theory and believed that what children read, including the books written for their pleasure and excitement by modern authors, pushed back the bounds of literary invention to complement their *deep* play.

I began to write about these things, not to start a new method of teaching reading with 'real books' as its shibboleth, but to explain what I learned when working with teachers who had resisted the lure of the single text of the reading scheme and instead had closely studied classroom interactions, describing their observations in words, not numbers. The publication of the Bullock Report in 1975 showed how children came to be writers. I'd hoped that it would reflect the influence of Frank Smith and Ken Goodman on views about reading, but the linear 'skills' model still prevailed in that otherwise important statement about the relation of language to learning. Later, when teachers began to appreciate the influence of texts on learning to read, there came the accusation that children were expected to become proficient 'by osmosis', and that the prevalent view was that they did not need to be taught. This was deliberate, distracting nonsense.

Some time after my own children had cleared the hurdle of learning to read in school, I took stock of the problems they had encountered. Their teachers had asked me not to 'teach' them because, they said, I might confuse them if my method did not coincide with that of the school. No one, however, could persuade me not to read to them. I watched their different styles as they tackled a range of different texts, their balance of fluency and accuracy, and what I have since learned to call their 'orchestration' of different kinds of knowledge, experience and attitude, as well as their purposive intent. They bolstered my unwavering conviction that children want to learn to read and will do so when their purposes are fully engaged and their imagination is captured in the world which the book presents to them, so long as they do not think that the enterprise is beyond them, or 'too hard'. They practise endlessly to become proficient when they see the point of what they are doing; they enjoy and extend their mastery in different ways as they grow in confidence and desire. I wrote *Learning to Read* to persuade parents and teachers that there was nothing so special about reading itself that they had to be able to do to help children to become experienced. But I know that the more anyone understands about the nature of the way language functions, and how texts teach, and what children enjoy, the more they can understand about the necessary complexity of reading acts. This is why I believe that there will never be enough time in the first professional learning time for teachers to make a full and flexible study of reading. As they continue to teach children they need to learn how children learn, from the children themselves, from their parents, and from those whose obligation it is to bring many of these things together in reflective understanding and research. The notion that teachers should be told by others who have only opinions and no knowledge about reading processes is false. My greatest regret, after a quarter of a century of working with teachers in the Institute of Education and in their schools, is the gradual disappearance of well-funded professional studies of the kind that invites teachers to bring their experiences to the scrutiny of theoretical understanding and the consequent revision of theory and practice. I have seen the great difference this makes. No one will now persuade me that it cost too much to let those whom I worked with read Vygotsky.

*

During the past ten years, arguments about reading have reflected our great unease and chronic indecisions about education. How much should all children have of it, what kind for some and others, who should pay for it? The installation of the National Curriculum, a frail net that tries to hold the system together, is the outward and visible sign of a political will to select the most able at an early age. Reading and writing are at the heart of the matter. On all sides there rise up fundamentalisms of different pedagogies, methods, texts and emphases, the clash of conflicting definitions, parental protest, teacher exhaustion. Why do we argue about the teaching of reading?

There are many reasons, each chosen by sectional interests to support a plan for social recovery in days of economic insecurity. The changes in our society and in our national identity are related to questions of 'access' to sources of information and the technological advantages these are believed to bring in their wake. Simply, reading and writing are not what they were in my days in the lamplit library. (I should perhaps tell you that I have taken refuge in the last one to be run by readers rather than ordered by machines.) In these days of electronic media, television and worldwide networks, learning to read in the primary school will not last for anyone's lifetime unless, and this is the real point, the learner discovers how to use reading as a way of *dialoguing with the future*. To be a part of a continuing identity in the reader, reading must be both flexible and reflexive. We have to investigate whose literacy counts; for now, as never before, reading and writing are about power.

At the heart of the current debates about reading standards is the problem not of how to teach it, but how to describe and assess it. As a nation we are still wedded to the notion that it is possible to make children heavier by weighing them. Again, opinion prevails over knowledge. The teachers who have come to record and to share with parents descriptions of a wide range of reading behaviours know that they are threatened not by alternative descriptions, but by forms of accountancy.

I still work with teachers who refuse to be cast down by what

I see as the wilful neglect of their understandings, and a refusal to grant them specialist status in this, the most important kind of schooled learning. There can surely be no going back from what we know, that the power of the reader lies in the interrogation of texts, the refusal to take for granted what is written in the manner of simple 'decoding'. The pervasive anti-intellectualism of English cultural behaviour has always included the idea that educating what the few have called 'the masses' is bound to be more threatening than creative. By thinking again of my Protestant roots, I know that this is false. Unless we redescribe reading and writing for all as the much needed source of our regeneration, we may well perish, stranded on a morass of examination papers and assessments of levels of attainment. Redescriptions begin by casting off the words that for too long have muddied our thinking about what reading is and cluttered our conceptions about how children learn to do it. I begin not with levels of correctness, decoding or skills, but with dialogue and desire.

BRENDA DEAN

'We need more women
to direct the kind of
society that we live in'

*Brenda Dean became the first woman general secretary of the Society
of Graphical and Allied Trades (SOGAT). During her period of
leading the union she had to deal with the Wapping dispute of 1986–7
and radical changes in the print industry. She left the union last year
after it merged with the National Graphical Association (NGA) to
become the Graphical Paper and Media Union (GMPU). She is now
chair of the Independent Committee for the Supervision of Standards
of Telephone Information Services.*

I didn't have a career structure, but if I had to single out one event
which got me going in an industry where men make all the top
decisions, it would be Ted Heath's Industrial Relations Act in
1971, which enraged me so much that I got up to speak at a meeting (only the second time I had ever done it and the first had been
to a prepared text), and brought the house down. It was a big open
meeting of paper mill workers and I just got up, terrified out of my
mind but fired by the desire to have my say. I had been the minutes
secretary of the SOGAT branch committee in Manchester before
that and had intervened at local committee meetings by asking a
question, because I formally wasn't allowed to speak. After that
things really took off and Bill Keys [the then general secretary of
SOGAT] asked me to join their panel of speakers. I think part
of my success was that the men never saw me as a threat and

I never saw myself as a threat; I had been their 'little' girl, and they were comfortable with me, protective of me and rather proud of this woman from Manchester who was getting up to speak. They were the older men who were coming up to retirement and really had nothing to worry about any more and they encouraged me. In a sense I became their mascot.

It must have been 1972 when I was elected assistant secretary of the branch. Until then it never occurred to me that I should stand for election, even though I was in the office every day, working with these men and in some cases actually doing their job for them, as a lot of secretaries do. When I was asked to stand for office I was doubtful about whether or not I could do it, but I decided to have a go. I later found out that behind the scenes there was a debate among the men about whether I was going to be a bit of a cold fish and too aloof. I was very shy and never messed around with any of them – I always kept them at an arm's length. I think my background helped me a lot because, as a kid, I was always told to be polite and respectful and listen when I was talked to and I think a lot of pushy women don't listen and that is part of their problem.

I never felt discriminated against, because the position of women being equal to men was never brought up in our family and I wasn't raised in a feminist environment; it was a case of grow up, get married and have two kids. It was never assumed I would have a career. I didn't have children. It just happened that way and I always say to the generation of women after me: 'Don't do what I did, don't concentrate on your career so much that you leave it too late to have children, if you want children. What the union wants out of you must fit in with what you want out of life, not the other way around.' I regret not having children, I regret it very much, but I don't feel heartbroken about it, I don't feel bitter, and if you look at women in my age group, with careers, it is quite common. I know that if I had had a family, I wouldn't have come this far and I think the biggest single change in the trade union movement is that, certainly in my union, most of the women officers now have children. Attitudes have changed and I would like to feel that by being a woman general secretary, I provided a role model while at the same time helping other women feel that they could remain within the organisation and still have children.

When I went to head office as number two to Bill Keys, one of our women staff became pregnant. It had never happened before and I mentioned to Bill that I couldn't find a copy of our maternity leave agreement. He was very pro-women but I was appalled to learn that we didn't have one. There we were, in 1983, arguing with the employers that they had to have maternity leave agreements and we didn't have one ourselves, because it had always been felt that the women were perfectly well looked after without one. We then got one of course and our whole negotiating agenda changed when I became general secretary.

It is critical to get women into positions of power in order to get issues like that addressed. I have always believed very strongly that if you make sure a woman's health is good, you don't just affect one person, you affect the whole family. In Manchester during International Women's Year I gathered around me a group of men and women from all walks of life, including the police (which got me in some trouble with the extremists), and we decided to do something permanent for the Women's National Cancer Control campaign, which was trying desperately to raise money for self-examination for early detection of breast cancer. I went to the branch meeting and asked if we could have £1000 and one man stood up and said: 'That's silly. We are the second biggest branch in the union, we'll give £2000' and off we went.

Then when I went to head office we conducted screening programmes for women and, even though there were still men who felt it had nothing to do with trade union activity, I got screening on the agenda for our national agreement. We had a really good negotiating committee with one or two younger men on board and we got it through: companies had to provide women with time off, without loss of pay, or provide the facilities on the plant. I negotiated it so that even if the women were non-union they got the benefit. Some of the men still said the employers had given us nothing, that it wasn't a benefit, but I regarded it as one of my achievements because it was aimed at women whose good health is

essential to family life. I know that if I had not been on the negotiating panel, it would not have been a priority. That is why you need
women in executive positions. You need the power to deliver, the
power to insist and the power to carry through, and sometimes you
can only do that if the buck stops at your desk. It might have got on
the agenda, but would it have been a priority? I can even remember
one Friday morning asking the employers for an adjournment and
taking their leader outside, which I could do as general secretary,
and saying: 'If you don't concede this you've got no agreement.' No
man, not even dear old Bill Keys, would have seen an agreement
breaking down over something like that.

We were at the point of getting childcare facilities in the last few
years but because of the recession that fell away. We pushed a lot of
equal pay for equal work cases through the courts, which is an
intensely frustrating business because you can't take a test case and
apply it to the whole industry. Moreover the employers will not
concede until their foot is in the courts, by which time the costs of
the industrial tribunal and the independent experts are enormous
and by which time the comparators you are using have disappeared,
or the women have given up. It is disgraceful really that we had
to go to court on nearly every case. It is about time someone wrote
an analytical work about the history of equal pay in Britain –
to expose the stumbling blocks that employers and the law have put
in the way of women and to demonstrate how much further we
need to go.

The whole quality of life for women under Labour's manifesto at
the last election would have changed; we would have felt in some
respects as if we were in a Socialist continental country with a new
vision. I think a lot of women feel we have slipped back a decade.
Mr Major is bringing women on in positions where the press can
look and say: 'Oh that's good, we've got a woman DPP now,' but
how many women judges have we got? Promoting women right at
the top only goes so far because it is the positions of power in-
between that count. We need more women to direct the kind of
society that we live in.

I suppose my greatest achievement was becoming the general secretary of a union that I thought would never elect a woman. When it happened I couldn't believe it myself; I was in my thirties, living out of London and a woman in a male-dominated union. I rationalised it as a vote for change which in a way reflected the image the trade unions had amongst their own members. The members were ready for a change. They felt that they had been dominated for too long by the Fleet Street image, they wanted to see things differently and they were given the chance to vote for that.

The fact that ballot papers very often simply have an initial, so that it isn't apparent that the candidate is a woman, is a big barrier to promoting women in unions. When I stood for president in 1983, I wrote to Bill Keys and said I wanted my nomination to say Brenda Dean and it did, but my God it created a fuss. London Central branch, the Fleet Street branch, wrote and said it was wrong and when I stood for general secretary the form said B. Dean, because they felt my name might have given me an advantage over the others.

I was switched off by feminism in the early 1970s and I wouldn't describe myself as a feminist in accordance with the public interpretation of the word. I am not one of the 'trendy Wendies' or a member of the chattering classes and I think that that image has done a lot of damage because, while the professional women have not done that badly, there are millions of women out there whose quality of life still needs improving. They are alienated and threatened by the feminist movement because they don't see 'feminists' as the kind of women that they want to become, yet it is their lives that we have to improve. Equal pay is one crucial way of doing that, but millions of women also lose out by giving through the whole of their active lives and then having to pay the penalty when they retire, because they have not built up any decent kind of pension, nor are they going to under this government which aims to shift everybody into personal pensions.

I am pleased to say that we have moved forward in trade unionism. We now have a network of women who weren't there before and who are changing the whole system in the sense that they are much more emancipated, but they realise that they have to relate to the women they are representing; they don't feel there is anything wrong with a woman being glamorous, for example, which is contrary to much of the feminist view in Britain, which has always seemed to teach that if you're glam you aren't a feminist. It is so important to have a role model right through every stratum of British life that women can relate to, in a dignified way, that gives them pride in themselves.

I probably did have quite a stern, tough image, which was necessary in negotiating, otherwise people would have said that because I was a woman, I was being a bit more soft than a man would be in that position. I didn't let that get at me but it was always at the back of my mind, so I had to set my own negotiating parameters because all the men's parameters were set out for them. They knew that a good way was to thump the table but I couldn't do that because I would have been a 'neurotic woman' if I had whereas if Bill, my predecessor, did it he was regarded as very strong. I was also very conscious that some men feel that because you are a woman you flirt, and I really couldn't do that in my job because the men on the other side of the table might have taken it in the wrong way.

Quite often in negotiations I would be the only woman in a room and that weighed on me quite heavily because I knew I could not expect the rest of the room to suddenly take on board my attitudes, so I had to find my own way, be straightforward and deal with the issues. I always felt it was incumbent on me to try and be informal, to make people feel at ease, even though I felt afterwards I had really put an added burden on myself. One of the few things that used to get to me when I was in the public eye was being compared with Mrs Thatcher because of my hair and my colouring. I never regarded Mrs Thatcher as being part of the network of women that I know. I didn't recognise any woman I knew in her. I know lots of women I don't agree with politically but there is always some strand of comradeship which cuts across traditional boundaries and demarcation, and that wasn't the case with her.

However I think after a while they stopped seeing me as a woman and I think that is why I got the job as general secretary of a union with a membership of 30 per cent women and 70 per cent men; people didn't feel when they put their cross by my name that they were voting for a woman because I had been around so long and had always talked about issues which affected men as well. I never forgot that there are a lot of men who are low paid and in Manchester one of my biggest achievements was working for the newspaper drivers, where the negotiations were often conducted through the night and I was representing groups of really quite chauvinistic men, some of whom were my greatest supporters.

I survived Wapping* through sheer stamina. I knew the dispute was going to happen, I knew I couldn't stop it and I think it is easier to cope with things if you have had time to think them through. Before it started I had had a fortnight's holiday over Christmas and New Year, all of which I spent thinking about it so when I came back there were no real shocks. I knew we would be sequestrated and I knew it would last at least three weeks or nine months, I knew there would be attempts to split the union and that my priority had to be to try and win the dispute if possible, and to keep the union together and not fall into the hands of some people within the movement who would have liked us to go bankrupt so they could take us over. The one thing I didn't countenance and which affected me because I was a woman, probably more than it affected my colleagues, was the impact on the families. That gradually built up and it was very wearing; marriages broke up, members died, the daughter of a young couple at a meeting fell through the staircase and died. I found that side of it was harder than any meeting with Mr Murdoch or our own people, some of

---

*The Wapping dispute arose because Rupert Murdoch did a deal with the electricians' union which allowed him to sack over five thousand print workers and still bring out his News International papers. The sackings coincided with News International's move to its new Wapping plant in London's East End in 1986.

which were very difficult because there was a lot of violence and at times my own personal safety was under threat.

I didn't get elected as general secretary of the new union, GPMU. I was prepared to give it a go as deputy as again, I didn't have the baggage that a man in my position would. I didn't personally regard not being elected as any kind of 'macho defeat'. Women are quite often good in number two positions and quite often not as disloyal as men in that situation, but it got to the point where I realised that I would have to say and do things that would damage the very thing I had created, because I didn't agree with a lot of what was going on.

My disagreement was a fundamental one. It wasn't one about tone, it was more about the downgrading of women's issues and health and safety, coupled with industrial policies which were like experiencing a 1960s time warp. There was a school of thought that was prepared to support my point of view, but at the end of the day I don't think I would have succeeded in reversing that and in the process I might have damaged not only what I had helped to create, but the leadership of the union and my integrity, so there was only one way forward and that was to leave. I wasn't bitter about what happened, I have seen so many people become bitter, and if I had become bitter it would only have affected one person and that would have been me; again it is all part of my background, you fall back into your basic values when you go through a traumatic period and I just thought it wasn't worth getting bitter about.

I would love to get my teeth into something else, but not necessarily a women's issue. I feel part of the key of achieving things for women is not to be a single-issue women's advocate and I think one of the reasons people said I spoke well for women was because I wasn't actually a representative of women; I was a representative of men and women. I would also now like to have a better quality of life than I have been having for the past decade.

I don't see any other predominant woman coming forward in the trade union movement in the immediate future. There are lots of women in the bottom and middle ranks but a lot of men who speak in favour of equality don't yet realise that it means them being pushed to one side. They think women will get jobs in addition to them, but they won't; a man has to go to make way for the women who are going to fill those positions. It is a tragedy that when I left the TUC General Council, there was no woman to step into my shoes. The union I came from had two representatives on the General Council and they were both women – we were the only union to have done it – but the new union doesn't have any women.

I am on the Opportunity 2000 target group and I think it is going to be quite positive. Companies have to carry out their own audits and then set their own targets for women, which means the chief executive has to be involved, and it is harder to say no to something they have set themselves than to something that has been set from outside. But Opportunity 2000 in the immediate future will only change the lives of women who are already doing quite well. If it brings on more women that will be something, but another thing I always say to younger women is: 'Beware women like me who have made it, and beware of thinking that because I have made it, so can you.' If Brenda Dean had been married at twenty and had produced a couple of kids and still become general secretary of the union (and quite possibly seen her marriage break up on the way) then we are motoring, but until then we aren't.

GAIL REBUCK

'Everything is set against the assumption that you have betrayed your sex'

Gail Rebuck helped to found the Century publishing company in 1982. After its merger with Hutchinson, the group was sold in 1989 to the American publishers Random House, of which she is now the UK chairman.

In publishing terms, mine is a very maverick career. I come from the last generation of graduates who assumed there would be jobs for them when they left university and never had a game plan. I didn't follow the traditional route of being a copy editor and would genuinely put my position now down to luck, and being in the right place at the right time.

I certainly don't come from a bookish family. Both my parents left school early. My father's parents were refugees from Latvia and my grandfather, who I never met, was a tailor in the East End of London who used to sell his suits from a wheelbarrow. He built up a successful family business so his children grew up as middle-class Jews. My mother's family also came from the East End. It was a difficult background and my mother had to go out to work to help support the other children. The work ethic was all in our family. You went out to make money in order to survive. Books and education were unnecessary in a strange way, although I was sent to a good school. I was about thirteen when someone said to me in passing: 'Well, I suppose you will apply to university?' It had simply never occurred to me before that. My love of books was a way of making sense of my background. My bedroom at home was the library.

I went to Sussex University and left with a degree in Intellectual History and French but no qualifications. I couldn't even type, but I never worried about my future. Nowadays the student culture is different and students are much more aware of getting degrees which might take them into the job market. I worked for an organisation which took American students around Europe, then went into business with my brother's girlfriend bringing antique clothes from the North and selling them in London where there was a big market. One day I found myself sitting in our shop in the King's Road in London, thinking about what the mark-up would be on a piece of antique clothing and realised I had to get out. So I took a six-week secretarial course to try and get a job in publishing. I was a production assistant in a children's publisher, an editor with a guidebook publisher and I ended up at Hamlyns with the job of starting up a non-fiction, mass market paperback list. The first book I bought was Susie Orbach's *Fat is a Feminist Issue* because I thought it was an interesting book. I read it and it spoke to me, and I assumed other people would find it interesting too.

A lot of success in publishing comes down to instinct, judgement and understanding how to put a book together. Being a paperback publisher is the best training because traditionally hard cover publishers looked at the intrinsic merits of the book, but not how to sell it. But we are in the 1990s now, and it is no longer a gentleman's industry. Marketing the book to the trade and the consumer is as important as the editor's skills. I had five years of list-building and complete freedom to make mistakes and to have some successes as well, which was a great training ground.

I became the chair of Random House at the end of 1991. It came as a huge shock to me to be asked to run the company. At that time I was in quite a senior position as chair of a division of the company. I was running my own little satellite but I didn't have that much to do with the corporate side. I felt I was plunging into a pool at the deep end and I wasn't entirely sure whether I was going to surface or not.

I was quite shocked by some of the reaction to my appointment. At first the press was quite sympathetic, but some time after I took over I gave an interview, which presented me in all the stereo-typical ways you could think of – as a ruthless, burningly ambitious woman, out to get to the top even if it meant trampling over people. My private life was scrutinised. It was especially upsetting as it was written by a woman journalist I liked. I don't think women journalists go around consciously trying to do other women down, but I think some unconsciously collude with the stereotype of a successful woman which is set up by men. Women executives are always described as tough. If they are not tough, then it is considered remarkable that they don't conform to this image of toughness. Everything is set against the basic assumption that you are a gorgon, that you have somehow betrayed your sex by taking on power, which some men find sits very unhappily on women's shoulders.

I think I am very direct and honest and cut through a lot of the machiavellian, charming, public school behaviour which typifies some male transactions in publishing. My meetings are often quite short, but some men find it very uncomfortable. They find that honesty threatening. Men are not socialised into having direct transactions, women are. If you have children and you work, there simply isn't time in the day to meander round a subject until you have got where you want to be. There is so much else to do at home that you want to get everything done at work as quickly and efficiently as possible.

Some men can also feel threatened if negotiations are not under-taken in a flirtatious way because they can't place you within the comfortable stereotypes that they have grown up with, and that must be unsettling. Directness is easier for younger men to handle than the older generation in business. I was even asked by one journalist, in his fifties, whether, when I was the only woman at the board table, I sensed a sexual tension. I had to tell him that was the last thing on my mind!

In fact I am quite the opposite to tough. I spend my entire life worrying about things. I know some ruthless and ambitious men who have walked into publishing companies and made sweeping changes with little regard for creativity, for authors or for culture. It has just been about the bottom line. I spend my life trying to balance creativity and profitability while also modernising the company. It is possible that some women in business get a bad reputation because they are generally in a minority around the board table, with a male chairman. A colleague once told me that in her company the men all tend to agree with the chairman because they want to be in his chair one day and the women are sitting there thinking they will never get there, so they might as well say what they think. That is something that comes up again and again when I talk to other successful women, most of whom usually put their success down to luck. I did not plan my career, which is why I don't recognise myself as a scheming ambitious woman, because I had no scheme. I had an ambition not to be bored and to be fulfilled in my working life; the minute I got bored I used to ask for something else to do. Younger women now do seem to plan their careers more but I don't know many women of my generation who did.

I think there is a need for senior women to get together now in support networks to get their self-esteem up. It may sound strange to people looking in from the outside, but most successful women I speak to admit that their self-esteem gets dented on a regular basis because there are no support systems. It happens because women have been socialised into wanting to be liked – the traditional role of a woman is to help and to please – but if you get into business, you sometimes have to make difficult decisions which can mean that you alienate people. Ironically the more senior you become, the more difficult the decisions and the more you can be disliked. The distance between you and all your old chums increases. So your self-esteem, which should be growing with your success, is in fact going the opposite way, not helped by the media caricature.

Of course the men have traditionally had a support network, and usually it is meeting at the time I am putting my children to bed.

When I was single and young I would think nothing of being in the pub until nine or ten at night, pulling the day apart. But I have two daughters now and my life is no longer centred around my work. My work has to fit in around my family commitments. It is very difficult balancing the two, especially in this job, because the stress levels are so much higher than anything else I have known. There are a lot of evening commitments, but I always try to be home for their bedtime and the weekends are for them alone. I used to feel a lot more guilty than I do now. I am all for women choosing but I do not believe that children are disadvantaged by having a working mother. If you have boys, you are changing their attitudes and with girls you are broadening their horizons.

KATE COSGROVE

'The national curriculum is a political stiletto'

Kate Cosgrove trained as an English teacher and is now the deputy head of Shaftesbury School in Dorset where she co-ordinates staff development and specialises in Personal and Social Education.

I have been teaching for almost twenty years, and in that time I have seen a lot of changes, starting with the raising of the school leaving age, which meant we picked up children who would previously been dubbed okay for factories and so on but were then expected to stay on at school an extra year. That was the first time everybody realised head-on that schooling had to be different and the shock of it hit everybody very, very hard. I suppose that really anticipated the changes that were to follow with the present government and the GGSE and so on.

I think a national curriculum which would help every child to have the standards of education that we would wish them has to be a good thing. Where I think the current national curriculum has gone very wrong is that it seems to be aping, to some extent, the European and American models and developing a strait-jacket in which every child who is learning English is going to be doing the same Shakespeare text or three Shakespeare texts in one year; that seems to me to be terribly prescriptive and limiting because I think one of the big advantages of our education system so far is that there has always been a reasonable amount of freedom and tolerant space for teachers to work with individuals and foster their own talents and their enthusiasm. Now if it is going to be as prescriptive as it seems to be, there is going to be less and less opportunity for doing that.

One of the things that is saddening at the moment, setting aside the chronic underfunding, is the expected rate of change that has been imposed on us; everyone is reeling because of the fact that we are expected to react to change at the same time as we are being expected to produce higher quality goods in the classroom. Everybody seems to be turning rather a blind eye to the fact that, if you want change, everybody has to be trained and would want to be trained, but every time you make a decision about doing that, either by going on a course or having some sort of training, you leave the classroom and the children, for whom we are there in the first place.

In my teaching subject, English, we have come to expect that every child will experience a wide range of experience in language and also a rich variety of literature, spanning all periods. During the last ten years of my teaching all students have experienced Shakespeare, and most have enjoyed sharing his view of human strength and frailty. The Key Stage 3 English curriculum* is a disaster. It is too prescriptive, it does not challenge either in its lack of variety or the lack of depth in the attainment tests, which only invite children to demonstrate by recall a minute part of what they know. Coursework allowed talent and enthusiasm to flourish, and so knowledge and skill to develop. Children and teachers had been given the reasonable freedom and tolerance to work as individuals. This opportunity is already dying.

The rhetoric of the Parents' Charter** disguises severe under-

---

* The National Curriculum is divided into ten key stages related to children's ages and levels of achievement.

** The Parents' Charter spells cut parental rights in relation to their children's education.

funding and now, in a more sinister manner, a very tight control exercised when funds are only given when practice is in accordance with central government objectives.

We all feel desperate about the rate of change imposed on us. There seems to be little recognition of the value of organic development, when one training initiative follows another so quickly. Good professional development usually is classroom-based, but this takes time. Rapid change necessitates rapid training which usually takes teachers away from the children in the classroom. Neither is it an argument to say teachers' holidays should be used for this training. Most teachers in my school are already working a day of twelve-plus hours. The pressure of performing in a classroom is at least as intense as that of an actor on stage, and so 'holidays' have to replace this lost energy and prepare for the next term.

This pressure also undermines successful teaching and learning. Curriculum overload, which is an attempt to deal with the complexity of living in the twentieth century, the simplistic levels of attainment at the key stages and the absurdly low-level modes of assessment proposed, deny both teacher and students the relaxed opportunity to explore and discuss the more controversial and challenging issues which promote real learning. The national curriculum is a political stiletto. There is no space to think or to explore in depth.

Success, we are told, lies in greater efficiency. Greater efficiency stems from more effective management. Effective management embraces careful strategic planning. How can I, and the management team of which I am a member, plan effectively when we have such limited forewarning of the curriculum we are to deliver, no knowledge of the budget we are to receive, no information as to how to staff subject areas whose nature we cannot anticipate? How can we deliver 'a broad and balanced curriculum' when we do not know what is required and what resources we are to have?

This has a particularly damaging effect on vulnerable areas such as equal opportunities. When money is short, part-time posts are the first to be axed. Many are usually held by women who also wish to retain the right to a family commitment. Women thus tend to be the first to lose their jobs. They are also less powerful in articulating their discontent, reinforcing their potential as a target. Opportunity 2000 seems to be a laudable initiative. With such support, it should be much easier to give women senior responsibilities in powerful management positions. Most schools in this country now have a stated commitment to an equal opportunities recruitment policy. The reality is that, increasingly, senior managers are males who are beginning to view a woman's appointment to a senior post with disguised concern. Education is an extraordinarily stressful job at present, and women who still tend to have the greater responsibility at home are at an obvious disadvantage in their capacity to cope well. Male management still seems to favour an aggressive, remote style and men still tend to promote candidates who represent their own image. The softer negotiating and supportive style offered by many women is still heavily patronised and disregarded.

Another route for women to progress in is now apparently being closed. In the 1970s and 1980s many women received middle-management allowances as senior pastoral heads. Women often entered senior management posts by that route. In schools there is increasingly less money for pastoral work as the core curriculum areas of English, maths and science are given a higher profile. It means that, for many women, there is no clear career path as the chief middle-management posts become less accessible to them. So I believe it will become far more difficult in practice for women to become deputy heads or headteachers.

This will offer a very poor role model to girl pupils, who tend to see women in less powerful posts now anyway. There will be *less* balance in management skills and expertise. It will also become more difficult for men to demonstrate these talents when the operational framework is becoming predominantly 'masculine' or 'macho'. This would be a catastrophe as many men are beginning to have the confidence to share and even to admit to a 'softer side' and family responsibilities!

Curriculum priorities are now governed by what the government demands, both in terms of its propaganda and the expectations thus created, and its legislation. While lip-service is paid to cross-curricular issues, I think that when the money is no longer there to support such development, issues such as equal opportunities will be increasingly marginalised.

Yet the notion of a charter implies that you have more choice for your child! You don't! You are likely to be getting considerably less in terms of effective teaching and support and a 'broad and balanced' education. Teachers and schools now have to operate according to the demands of a market economy without the means to deliver effectively or attractively what its 'customers' require.

The good that may develop from all this is the notion of flexibility. Individuals, institutions and communities are beginning to realise the importance of creating different answers. A flexible day, where your core curriculum occupies the main teaching space, could be offered, with an extended curriculum timetabled across the afternoon and evening. This would also attract adults from the community and offers an imaginative and not impossible way forward. Supported self-study for senior pupils adds to this potential, as does the development and refinement of the possibilities created through information technology and resource-based learning.

Here you recognise that education extends throughout an individual's life and you optimise the use of a school's facilities. You also enhance people's potential to be committed to their job *and* their home and family. A radical solution, perhaps, but I feel passionately that the polemic has to cease and that an imaginative and co-operative response must develop in answer.

I worry that although parents want their children to be happy and successful at school, they seem to have little perception of the freedoms and the opportunities which are being eroded. The appeal of the notion of a national curriculum which creates opportunity masquerades as a brilliant and achievable possibility. In my view, it is hiding the erosion of an opportunity to be equal that we have come to take for granted over the last twenty years. It can only be met with radical alternatives.

ELIZABETH MacLENNAN

'A cold reactionary wind blowing from the south'

Elizabeth MacLennan is an actress who was one of the originators of 7:84 Theatre Company which pioneered popular political theatre throughout England and Scotland and Wales in the 1970s and 1980s.

I grew up in Glasgow with strong roots in the Highlands. My parents were both doctors. It was a professional middle-class background but it would be impossible for anyone with a mind and a Scottish education to grow up there and be unaware of the contradictions in society. Although my father was a Tory, I would describe his political position as roughly equivalent to today's Liberal Democrats and probably more radical than today's Labour Party. Both my parents were passionately committed to the National Health Service. They would be appalled at what is being done to it today. My father – a gynaecologist – did research into contracted pelvis in the 1930s and was acutely aware of the relationship between health, housing and poverty. My mother was a socialist, worked in public health and was very involved in preventative medicine. Diseases like TB that they struggled to eradicate at that time are now alarmingly on the increase. The position of women at work and in health terms has deteriorated in a way she would have abhorred.

Having considered medicine myself, my first thought was to be a pianist like my granny. Music is still important to me. But I started acting at school, and I always was a mimic. At Oxford University I read history and became involved with all kinds of experimental theatre. I have always been drawn to new styles and techniques, new plays, new writers. It was a very energetic, talented generation. I wanted to be part of a theatre company where music, ideas, entertainment, people and passion were paramount. I worked in repertory, television and films, gaining experience and a lot of good parts in the next ten years. When we started our own company, 7:84 Theatre Company, in 1971 we all shared the idea that people actually do go to the theatre to have a good time! And that it is a shared experience rather than something *you* do to *them*. We wanted too to make people think about our society, but always using humour and music and character – 'real' characters as well as caricature. We were planning this during the late 1960s when a lot of new theatre buildings were going up and public funding for the arts was increased remarkably by Jennie Lee, the then Arts Minister under a Labour administration.

But we felt that a new building wasn't the answer for us. We wanted to reach out to the places where theatre wasn't widely available at that time. We wanted to take theatre in the popular tradition with high production standards and skills which would also answer or face up to some of the questions that people are concerned about in their own lives. We gradually built up a network of places to play – universities, village halls, community centres, town halls, schools, trade union clubs, miners' clubs, big theatres, factories. We travelled in two vans all over England, Scotland, Ireland, Wales and parts of Europe, Canada and the USSR, for seventeen years. It was exhausting, but exhilarating, and we were learning all the time. We developed a loyal audience and an ongoing dialogue. Many talented players, writers, directors, designers and technicians came on board. We worked on the basis of collective decision-making and equal pay, although the organisational structure did vary from company to company.

Most families never go near the theatre except perhaps at Christmas time for the panto. At that time, and still to a large extent, a great deal of theatre was and is exclusive. It happens in buildings which are often intimidating with impersonal glass-fronted foyers, impenetrable booking systems and *is* too expensive. We wanted – along with many theatre makers of my generation – to break down those barriers. To welcome people. To do shows that were relevant and at the same time provide a good night out. This has to a large extent influenced the way many theatres are now run. But it was quite revolutionary.

Now, with government and local authority cuts, all these kinds of initiatives are struggling and already many of the communities where we played and the local organisations who supported us, are decimated.

There were, of course, other companies who were very active in this way. Most of them were destroyed by the cuts so euphemistically described in 'The Glory of the Garden' (Arts Council policy document, 1984), which napalmed the seed beds nurturing talent and new audiences; the few that remain today are already next in line (Stoke on Trent, Liverpool Everyman etc). But the establishment/mainstream theatre favoured and still does favour a theatre which is comfortable, expensive, nostalgic and slightly boring; preferably starring well-known TV personalities and which doesn't hold any danger. Nevertheless we continued to tour to big audiences and perform a number of the plays on television as well right through until the mid 1980s. But along with may other folk we faced quite brutal and heavy opposition in trying to stay alive as a company. There was a cold reactionary wind blowing from the south. Margaret Thatcher was accomplishing her long march through the institutions and we found ourselves increasingly embattled. In 1984 the English 7:84 was cut by the Arts Council with no appeal. Four years later they tried to do the same in Scotland, and more or less succeeded. There *was* a difference between us and some so called 'agit prop' companies. We had managed not to become marginalised, particularly in Scotland where we remained very popular with audiences, and so of course were not desirable from the Tory point of view. They were perplexed that audiences loved us, and that audiences loved the

English company all over the north of England; it provided a kind of rallying point for articulate opposition.

A piece of theatre in its time *can* affect the consciousness of a whole country. John McGrath's *The Cheviot, the Stag and the Black Black Oil* (1973) changed the political climate in Scotland. It also changed the practice of popular theatre. A number of other 7:84 shows were highly effective in support of values and working-class struggles and women's struggles that were threatened in the 1980s and are even more so today. I am very aware of being part of a movement which is under severe duress throughout the world and while I feel very sympathetic to the theatre groups that are now struggling to survive in this country, I also think of companies who are working today in South Africa, for example, and in Chile and Nicaragua working under even greater financial and political stress. But theatre as a way of giving voice to popular feelings will never be silenced in spite of today's chill winds.

I feel quite schizophrenic because of being Scottish and living and working in both Scotland and England. There is such a different culture. I am totally committed to the idea of a Scottish Parliament because in Scotland we are not represented by the government that sits on us and we haven't been for decades. It is not just that we haven't got the government we voted for – it is a different mentality, a different country, different culture, different language. Within England itself there are many different divisions. It is possible to speak to the whole of Scotland, whereas it is very difficult to speak to the whole of England. I don't think the English really know who they are. At the moment there is projected a kind of illusion of Englishness based on nineteenth-century values and a long-gone empire, with regiments and afternoon tea and world prestige, and big hats and 'Made in Britain', with a 'special relationship' with the United States, and with convincing royalty and loyal all-white subjects. It's an illusion which is masking the most secretive, repressive and pre-fascist government in decades. And so far the opposition in England seems incapable of dealing with it in any coherent way, although we all know it is illusory. There are other urgent common political themes for our present times which reach out beyond national boundaries, like the current sense of bereavement and disempowerment for dissenters and those on the left.

I did a one-woman show last year in London, Edinburgh, Glasgow, St Etienne and Bologna called *Watching for Dolphins*. It was written by John McGrath and dealt with the position of a feminist who finds herself aged fifty-two, having spent a lifetime as an activist, with her whole world turning upside-down due to the collapse of the 'communist world' and 'at the end of history'; how does she proceed when all the ideological ground is falling apart? It is a brave play and I worked very hard on it. It is brave because it doesn't shirk any of the difficult questions which that generation has to face, or indeed anybody who wants to keep politically active at a time when socialism has been so systematically discredited throughout the world, has to face. It is not loss of faith, it is about bereavement and questioning, and there are many people of that generation who feel that way. When I started doing the play a year ago I felt quite isolated in it, as though I was sticking my head out of a port-hole in a hurricane. After the election suddenly there were many people who felt the same way. They understood what we were talking about and that is becoming true all over Europe. While so much that has been swept away was repressive, it has not been replaced by a more democratic open world. Indeed fascism is growing throughout Europe at an alarming rate, And still 7 per cent of the world owns 84 per cent of the wealth, and keep the rest starving and wretched, and women are still suffering the most.

I played *Dolphins* recently at a European summer school in Edinburgh with Croats, Chinese, Bulgarians, Africans, English and Americans in the audience. After we finished the whole audience stayed to talk about their respective positions in the world – and how they could face this hurricane of change. It was very interesting. At the Citizens Theatre in Glasgow the discussion was spontaneous and exciting and urgent. There has never been a more pressing time for popular political theatre to address the problems that face us.

CLAIRE RAYNER

'Romantic love is too high up the agenda'

Claire Rayner is a former nurse who became a writer, television personality and agony aunt for newspaper and television

I sometimes feel that society is coming full circle. I was a child in the East End before the war and remember what poverty was like – children starving, at school in clothes that didn't fit them, a lot of single parents, because people died young and of course during and after the war half the kids at school didn't have fathers. I used to get angry about things quite early on. My first political act was discovering as an evacuee that I could run away and I ran away a lot and used to get beaten for it. A lot of my anger from then stayed inside me. I became a nurse and a midwife in the 1950s. In those days 40 per cent of deliveries were done at home – that was the rule – but you could go into hospital with the first baby or if there were problems. Magazines were full of articles about 'How to get yourself into hospital' because women didn't want to stay at home. I learned a lot being a midwife and a lot of it horrified me. I laid out the body of a girl who died in her own bed because she had the baby at home – the baby died too. If she had been delivered in hospital it would have been all right. But it was great fun 'doing the district' on a great big bicycle with a big black bag swaying from the handles down the Old Kent Road. They were marvellous people and in those days doctors, and to an extent nurses, were the aristocrats to the working class.

Des turned up when I was twenty-five. He wanted to get married, I was a staff nurse and he was an out-of-work actor. He was quite right to want to be married because I'm a bolter – if things aren't right I cut loose and cut my losses. I think at the back of my mind was the thought that I daren't risk doing to any child what was done to me. Anyway I did marry and started my career with a book about the maternity services and it just took off from there. Des was wonderfully supportive, he made me go on when I thought of giving the writing up, but I still found myself asking him if he was sure about it because I had grown up with the notion that if your husband didn't want you to do a thing, you shouldn't do it. I have always said I married a 'new man'. From the word go, if he was home he did the housework and if I was home I did it. I used to work Saturday mornings and he didn't and he always had bits of laundry done and the lunch cooked and when the children were young he would get up and give them a bottle in the night on Friday and Saturday so I could be sure of having three or four nights' sleep. He was terrific.

Is there such a thing as a new man now? No, I think there is a selfish man and a sensible man and there always has been. I just think there are more sensible men today – more women have reared sensible people. When we first married, Des would actually go out and not think anything of pushing the pram or being seen carrying flowers, which wasn't done in the fifties. Now we go to our local supermarket and you see fathers with the kids, talking to them with their shopping list, obviously giving mother the morning off.

There is also an idea around today that the nuclear family is disintegrating. But it was never real in the first place. Thatcher's view of the family was a television or magazine advertisement. She embodied in it what she had seen in the Oxo and Ovaltine ads with the fire and the children playing games and dad smoking a pipe. One in three families now is headed by a woman and, in all fairness, a great many households were headed by women in the forties and fifties. I can remember seeing families in which the husband used to come home on Friday and put his unopened pay packet on the table, his wife would take it and open it and give him back his pocket money, while she had a row of tins in the kitchen for the different family expenses. I think the conventional family was matriarchal to a much larger degree than people realised and many of the mothers I looked after when I was nursing in north London were single mothers in real terms. They had men who came home, had a meal and then went out to the pub, then came back for their sex and slept away a Sunday afternoon while she did all the work. But at least somebody came home, and they had someone to wash socks for and being needed is very important.

There is a huge mythology about single parents today, yet they're nothing new. There were vast numbers of widows after the war. People forget how many children grew up without fathers. I was virtually in a one-parent family because my father didn't come back until 1945 – he'd gone in 1939. I think the difference today is that a lot of men have lost their guilt about not looking after their wives. A chap was measured as a provider then, now they've stopped worrying about being providers because to an extent there is a cushion, in the form of the welfare state, on which the men think the old woman can land. I hate to say that because I feel so desperately about the state caring for people but some people seem less willing than they might be to accept their responsibilities.

A lot of the underlying problems are the same as they were when I started as an agony aunt. A girl would write to me in the fifties and say: 'I'm pregnant and I don't want to be; where can I get it adopted?' Then in the sixties it was 'I'm pregnant, I don't want to be, where can I get an abortion?' Then in the 1980s and 1990s it became 'I'm pregnant, I don't want to be, but what benefits can I get to help me rear the baby alone?' The basic problem – unwanted pregnancy – hasn't changed an iota. In spite of attempts to provide lots of sex education and adequate contraception.

The commonest problem I see is people not talking enough, not saying what they really mean, not listening; nobody knows how to listen to what is being said, they only listen to the words, not the feelings or the space in between the words and the questions that aren't asked. Social changes have meant a lot but they still haven't altered the fact that we all live in little glass boxes and there is a desperate hunger, an increasing hunger for closeness and idealised romance. If you look at the 1920s and 1930s the images of relationships in popular entertainment weren't as intense. Whereas our grandmothers would have said: 'He's not a bad husband, he doesn't beat me, he gives me my wages regularly,' today the same woman would say within a very short time: 'I don't know what has gone wrong with my marriage, all the glamour has gone out of it.' Romantic love is too high up the agenda. It is a mistake to think that one person can satisfy all your needs. Des is heaven but if I tried to get all my needs out of him it would be impossible, yet that is what people seem to expect from their relationships. I always say don't think everyone has the right to happiness or to be loved. Even the Americans have written into their constitution that you have the right to the 'pursuit of happiness'. You have the right to try but that is all.

CHRISTINE CRAWLEY

'There is a "behind the hand" giggle if you mention "women's issues" in the House of Commons'

Christine Crawley has been a Labour Member of the European Parliament for nine years. She now chairs the Women's Rights Committee which has campaigned vigorously to get equal opportunities proposals through the Parliament.

I come from a local government background where I used to get great satisfaction from people coming and asking me, what are you going to do about my drains, or where am I on the housing list? It meant being close to people's needs. By contrast, moving to European politics seemed suddenly being quite a long way from local demands and distant from what people see as being most relevant to their everyday lives. However, that didn't last long, as I made sure that every campaign on a European theme which I instigated was anchored as locally as possible. I don't regret going for a European seat at all. I did try for Westminster first in 1983, but didn't succeed and so by the time the selection process for the European Parliament came along, I was already up and running in election mode, so I had an attempt at the most marginal seat in the United Kingdom which had a 500 Conservative majority. We turned it round to a Labour majority of 21,000 and then at the last European election, my seat had a 48,000 majority.

I did make an attempt at one stage to go from the European Parliament to Westminster but I now think the job to be done in

Europe is more important than ever. We can't operate economically as a single nation state any longer. We have over 60 per cent of our trade with Europe so our future is obviously as part of Europe. The European Parliament is becoming a much better forum for women – there are now 100 women MEPs out of 518 here – it isn't as adversarial as the House of Commons and there wasn't an obstacle, for example, to setting up a Women's Rights Committee across the political parties which I chair and which has been a standing permanent committee of the Parliament since 1984 and is highly valued for having a very positive role to play in acting as midwife to equal opportunities proposals that have come from the EC since then. I don't know whether it would be possible to set up a similar committee at Westminster today. I presume not, otherwise it would have happened by now. There is a 'behind the hand' giggle if you mention 'women's issues' in the House of Commons which owes a lot to its public school ethos. I truly admire the women MPs who organise and battle against the prejudice in the House of Commons. That class thing doesn't exist in the European Parliament. You don't get that awful feeling of hierarchy that comes through, even to an outsider, at Westminster.

The issue of equal opportunities could really have taken off in the 1990s if we had a government which was really participating in Europe, but British women have been sacrificed in the government's decision to remain outside the Social Chapter of the Maastricht Treaty which, if we had opted into it, would have given new impetus to the areas of health and safety at work, decent pension rights and EC policies of equal opportunities. Another government – a Labour government – in the future will take us back fully into the Maastricht Treaty, which is why I feel it is better to have a treaty – with all its problems – rather than have no regulating forward plan for Europe in the 1990s. As it is, the other European countries will benefit from social directives which encourage sharing work and home life. The Parental Leave Directive that gives men and women time off work within the law to look after children who are sick or disabled can now be passed by a majority vote of the Council of Ministers, but

Britain will be excluded from taking part at the request of our government.

Both Thatcher and Major's attitude towards Europe has been very cynical – it has simply been about having a free trade zone, a commercial deal which enables Britain as a country to benefit from a simple trading market. Beyond that they are basically not interested. The government pays lip-service to the environmental aspects of EC policy, pays less than lip-service to overseas aid and it blocks and disrupts as much on equal opportunities and workers' rights as possible. This is not so much a 'hands off' attitude as a 'shoulders shrugged' attitude to our membership of the EC. They just don't believe it is relevant. The only thing you can say about their attitude is that it is consistent. Britain has been consistently dragged into taking action on issues like equal pay by Europe, although we are a long way from achieving it as women are still taking home up to 32 per cent less pay than men for doing work of a similar value. In spite of repeated opposition from Britain, a directive on maternity leave has finally come through which will become law and which will help 150,000 British women. I am proud of the work we have done in the European Parliament and especially in the Women's Rights Committee on this important directive. It won't actually affect a lot of other European women who already have much better maternity rights than this directive established, but because our British maternity rights are so abysmal, it will pull us up to somewhere near the European average. We have one of the worst childcare records in the European Community, along with Portugal and Greece, and we are right down at the bottom of the league on child benefit, with Denmark, Germany and France way at the top. The British government is seriously reactionary towards what the public purse can do to help get a better balance between men and women's contribution at home and work.

The Women's Rights Committee is drawing up a report in central and eastern Europe and one of the real problems there is that women are almost invisible in the new regimes and the new democracies that have arisen from the ashes of the old, discredited

Eastern bloc. The new democracies have not thrown up groups of women who are demanding better training, better job protection and the right to improved childcare arrangements – quite the opposite, in fact. We are seeing very few women in these new parliaments, we are seeing a lot of the childcare arrangements that had existed before and were publicly funded, collapsing – partly because they were tied to jobs which are collapsing. So women in the most vulnerable work sectors are losing jobs first and then losing childcare facilities as public spending is being cut back. I've heard male MPs from central and eastern European countries saying, 'Why do we need a large public spending programme for child benefit and sick pay and so on while there are all these unemployed women who can look after the children and the old people?' It is a sad logic but what they are saying is that our countries are poor, we have hyperinflation, we can't afford public spending and just look at all these unemployed women – they can do the caring now. It is dire for a lot of women – a move back in time; just when freedom should have been moving them forward.

On top of all that there are the ethical issues, such as a woman's right to choice in matters of contraception and abortion. The Parliament in Poland is very influenced by the church and has recently imposed radical restrictions on the availability of abortion. On top of that, contraception is not available because it is too costly so women are threatened on all fronts. They are worse off than they were before in many cases – stuck at home without a job, without employment benefit and often they are looking after children and an unemployed husband and other dependent relatives.

We are currently looking at the funding programmes that the Community already has up and running with central and eastern European countries and we are trying to ring fence funds for women. For instance the PHARE fund, which aims to facilitate new democratic systems of local government and new structures to replace the old centralised system, is insisting that women must be involved in building these new structures. They must also receive training to work in these new structures and we are calling for a clear account of exactly how much training money goes to women in central and eastern Europe. We are also giving sisterly solidarity to women by organising reciprocal gatherings between women in the Community countries and in central and eastern Europe to try and share experiences and support new democratic systems.

The next major task of the European Parliament's Women's Rights Committee is to organise an international public hearing on the rape of women in the former Yugoslavia. We must end this terrible abuse; European governments cannot be passive spectators while rape is being used as a weapon of war against thousands of women and children.

I am ultimately optimistic about Europe's future. However, I believe that because we are in a recession, and in this country a slump, it makes any debate about Europe and countries beyond the UK very much more difficult to conduct. British people are obviously and quite reasonably more worried about jobs, their homes and their own lives at present than what is going on in Europe and they will always be inward-looking when there is mass unemployment. Fourteen years of a Tory government has left people in this country with such low expectations, I find myself permanently having to say: 'You don't have to expect this level of bad childcare, you don't have to accept this level of maternity allowance – they don't accept it in Denmark or Sweden.' Yet I know it is possible to raise people's sights. We have seen it being done in the debate over pensions. Pensioners in this country now know exactly what pensioners are getting in Germany, Italy and Spain, and they have become one of the most strong and vociferous lobby groups because of that. Giving people information about what is going on in other countries can give them some hope and that is one of our biggest tasks.

How many British women know about the existence of women's ministries in other countries, for instance, and that they have been accepted in Europe for some years now? Admittedly there are different types. France has got a very strong women's ministry, Denmark has one as part of the employment ministry. Spain has an Institute of Women which has on its board ministers from the government who can therefore see the relevance of all their policies on women. In Ireland, when there was a women's ministry, it was part of the Cabinet Office – but it is now funded differently and has a different status in government. It is fascinating to compare this activity with the Committee for Women's Issues established by the Conservative government.

In spite of my original intention to become a Westminster MP, working in Europe has grown on me. The hardest part of doing this job for a woman is the guilt of not being with your family enough which you carry around like a knapsack on your back because of the time you have to spend abroad. In the end you learn to live with it and work at making time together, which is special family time. I have been an MEP for nine years and the distance was more problematic when the children were smaller. They are now in their late teens but when they were younger it was often a case of trying to sort out PE equipment and whether or not they had remembered to take in their dinner money to school over the phone from Brussels!

It is always with hindsight that you are wise and the work did affect my personal life and my health some five years ago. Although we are divorced now, my ex-husband and I remain very good friends and he has always been extremely helpful and supportive. We share the upbringing of the children, his role being the home-base parent, when I am away. I recently remarried and was proud to share the day with my beautiful, sensible, good-humoured children. Perhaps it's not impossible to do a rather unusual international job like mine and still keep close as a family.

HILARY ROWLANDS

'The miners' strike was a turning point for me'

Hilary Rowlands is a former school dinner supervisor living in Markham in the Sirhowy valley of South Wales. She has been a member of the Labour Party since her early twenties and took a leading part in the local women's support group during the miners' strike of 1984–5. She is doing a degree and is a member of Islwyn Borough Council.

The miners' strike was a turning point for me. I think that is when I really started to gain confidence. I was so angry. I knew I had to do something and the confidence just grew from there. It was a collective organisation of women and that brought us into conflict with the men in the local miners' lodge because they wouldn't let us go picketing. We couldn't do anything without asking the committee. Eventually we started to part from the committee, particularly because we thought the miners' children should have their own Christmas party because they had been without for longer, but the committee thought that *every* child in the three villages should be at this party. They demanded money off us, money we had begun to collect and donations we had been given, but we just went out and spent it before anyone else could so that every miner's child had a present. We went and bought boxes of fruit and sweets so that we could add those to the food parcels.

I never really got to find out why they resented us doing our own thing but they may have thought we were going to take their power away and they felt we knew nothing about the situation and should just be in the background. It was all right for us to go and collect food and go door-to-door collecting money but, oh no, we couldn't go on the picket lines.I don't think they thought it was undignified for women, I think they were afraid of our growing influence and strength. So we just split off and continued raising funds, collecting food wherever we could.

Before that I had just worked in the school canteen and after it was all over there was the feeling that things couldn't be the same again. I think the majority just went back into their homes or their workplaces and you heard or saw nothing of them. I was already politically active. That had been my upbringing and I think I realised my own value. I have always considered myself equal, but I never had the confidence to act as if I was. It was only during the strike that I properly realised that because I was a woman, I was separate. The men defined it for me by saying we couldn't go and picket. I thought, you can go into the Labour Party and be accepted as an equal, but you can't go to the pit lodge and be accepted. We were women and they didn't mind taking the money we collected or the food we collected, but that is all that was expected of us.

There is no hope for the kids here now. None whatsoever. To be honest, I'm frightened. My son Barry has been out of work since July. Although I have always realised how bad it is, there comes a time when it knocks on your own door and you really get scared. It is worrying because it does put strain on the families. We are used to the boys being out at work and when everybody is here lolling about it is stressful. I've got to keep working. Barry has even said he would go abroad to work, but where do you go? Why should families be split up like this anyway? He gets £33.40 a week from the social security. He has never before been out of work.

We are struggling and I've got to clothe him as well as feed him – he didn't ask to be made unemployed. There are water rates, poll tax and at the end we are left with about £20 to buy food and that is not pleading poverty. I'm not the only one going through it. I have never known it as difficult as it is now and I'm not hopeful at all that things will get better. I am really fearful. I was devastated by the election. There was a real gloom in the village – nobody could believe how selfish people could be – they didn't have the good heart to try something different to give us a chance. I try telling people – they'll never give us a chance. When the Tories are talking they are not talking to us, they couldn't care less about us. I firmly believe that.

The government has no idea whatsoever of how we live and they are not particularly interested in finding out. There is this idea that everybody has to fend for themselves – you just can't. You can't be an individual, have real freedom, unless you are part of a collective – because that is the only way you have got protection and support. You can't afford to be anything now. I decided to go the University of Glamorgan but was too old to get a student loan because you have to apply before you are fifty and I enrolled the day after I was fifty so you are penalised for wanting to do something which might help to get a job or just make you better educated. I'll be just coming up to fifty-three when I finish – so I don't consider myself old. I regret not having done it years before but I intend getting a job and using my degree to help myself and some other people, too, I hope.

It was Neil [Kinnock] who made me believe I could go back into education. He always encouraged me to develop my abilities. Without him I would never have had the confidence to think of myself as capable of becoming an undergraduate. It was a big step for me to take, but I know it has been worth it.

Do I think of myself as a feminist? Not really. I agree with a lot of what they say. I've fought for women and during the miners' strike I had to fight because I was a woman. I can see that women are oppressed but I think women are generally too busy bringing up children, taking on part-time work or sorting out the family to rise up. They need confidence and I totally support women's sections because they are places where you can start off. If you can get a woman into the Labour Party through a women's section that is where their confidence comes from. We haven't come very far, to be honest. A man goes out to work – I don't know how much he gets involved in the union now – but they are with colleagues all day, talking all day, discussing what is in the papers, on the news, what about this and that. But a woman is at home – she might go to the shop but you don't see women stopping and discussing big issues. They'll talk about Andy and Fergie and Di and Charles. You hear men complaining about this bloody government but you never hear women stand and talk like that. It is a man's world.

But I feel that now I am capable of getting up and doing something about it. Most women won't take up direct action. If you couldn't get them to stick together with the poll tax, they won't stick together over anything. There are women in Wales being ruthlessly exploited, getting paid a penny for making a cracker which takes hours and hours to do. It is slave labour but they just keep at it and don't rise up.

Being on the council gives me no pleasure, but I just have to do it. The people in the village are marvellous and if I can manage to get something done they are very grateful. But with all the cuts and controls there is no real power to make changes that are needed. There's no joy in being a councillor, because you can't give people what they want, what they need or what they deserve.

INEZ McCORMACK

'They're responsible for hospital hygiene – they don't "just clean"

Inez McCormack is the District Secretary for UNISON in Northern Ireland. She was the first woman officer in the union and the first woman from Northern Ireland ever elected to the Executive Council of Irish Congress.

The core of my work is not about people putting in pay claims, rather it is about enabling women to have more confidence in themselves and to value themselves, which for many women is not the prime thing on their minds. Many women take part-time jobs in early morning or late at night to fit in with family pressures, so their main preoccupation is minding their kids, minding their husbands, minding everybody except themselves. The important thing for me is to try to get them to take some space for themselves as a first step to looking at who they are, where they are in their work patterns and where they are in life. For that to happen women need to be organised in a way that enables them to raise issues that are important to them. Those issues are not necessarily work issues – indeed one of the most effective topics we have found around which to organise women is that of woman's health. Initially women express surprise that a union should be interested in such things. When they realise that we have placed some value on them they begin to place more value on themselves.

Some other issues help to do that. We may not have achieved

equal pay or equal value for work done, but these are mobilising words and in one hospital we brought hundreds of women together when they began to think about their rate of pay and suddenly realised that they were at the bottom of eighteen pay grades set not by God, but by employers and male trade union officials. The women started to get very annoyed and I have a wonderful memory of hundreds of them filling in industrial tribunal forms for equal pay even though they understood very clearly that they might not win. It wasn't a question of winning or losing but of affirming who they were, and from that began a discussion about what they did. Back then if you asked a women what she did, she would invariably say 'I just clean'. If you pressed her she would go into more detail. You would then discover, as we did, that she might clean in the maternity hospital, had done so for years and spent two or three hours a day doing things such as dismantling incubators, putting them together again, to ensure sterility in order that babies could survive. So she was responsible for hygiene – she didn't just clean. But because cleaning and caring are regarded in the private sphere as women's jobs which don't really matter, when they are translated into the public sphere they are undervalued jobs.

The really important thing about the equal value tactic was that once women had placed some worth on themselves it enabled them to challenge, both through the collective bargaining structure in the union and through the courts. They understand very clearly the value of putting pressure on the boss from as many angles as possible.

My activist background is in civil rights in the 1960s. Feminism came later and formed my thinking and taught me how to organise. The women part-time workers I represent come from some of the toughest ghettos in Northern Ireland. They are not weak, they are strong women, but at the bottom of every scale, extremely badly paid, and were unorganised. Tackling that meant working out what was important to them and it was quite often the smaller issues in trade union terms, the issues that didn't have names like being hassled by your supervisor at work or sexual harassment which has a name now, but didn't fifteen years ago. All the work we have done, whether on pay or conditions or on health or education, has been about power relationships and about transforming a person's view of themselves in order to transform the power relationship in which they work and live. Just getting someone a pay rise or equal pay or minimum wage doesn't change the power relationship within their workplace. Mobilising them does. Some of the equal pay cases are now nine years in court, so they do nothing about changing women's lives or women's pay but they do something about changing women's view of themselves. My attitude to employers is, 'Mobilise all this energy, see that these women aren't treated as skivvies, use their talents and abilities, train them, reorganise them, see them as part of a team. If you don't do that, we will take industrial action and we will take legal action.'

In that way women who are used to being humiliated by doctors who trip over them in the corridors and physically don't see them, never get tripped over again. A decade ago you couldn't get women night workers to come to a meeting, because they felt they would come under pressure. I have a vivid memory of one of our women night workers being disciplined for speaking out. She was summoned to a hearing. In the early days it would have just been her and the shop steward with the members waiting at the end of the corridor to see what happened. This woman was part of a group of mobilised women and hundreds of other women poured into the meeting with her. The view was simple: touch one of us and you touch all of us.

Organising some kinds of workers, like home helps, is more of a challenge. They are people who have traditionally been seen as impossible to organise because they are casual workers with no set workplace. It took me twelve years to go from seven in membership to two and a half thousand and I did it by putting notices outside post offices advertising a meeting in the community centre that night. I would get to the meeting and five or six people would turn up.

But I wrote to them all asking them to pass letters down the street, getting people to come to other meetings, finding out where the bingo sessions were and going half an hour before and half an hour afterwards, finding out who took the old people's pension on a Tuesday morning and standing outside the post office and recruiting them as they went in. By going to them, they worked out that we were serious, but it takes a lot for women to be organised in large bureaucratic organisations that can simply regard them as a means to an end rather than looking at their worries as a priority.

You have to organise them in a way which recognises the fact they they live life in a hurry. If you see a home help she is usually carrying two plastic bags – one for herself and one for her client – rushing to get her work done.

The majority of part-time workers live life in a hurry. Hurrying to get the kids, hurrying to get home. The 'hurry' needs to be addressed. I often say 'Walk, don't run.' They beam when I say that because I have addressed the fact that they have a right to walk – I put some value on them and they put some value on themselves.

I've had many battles with my own movement but I still regard it as my movement. The reaction within unions to the notion of putting value on these kinds of women has changed radically over the years. It has moved from 'Don't be silly, Inez' to 'Very good, Inez', but is only now being take seriously. What has changed however are the financial imperatives. Women have always been in the work-force but they are now there in large numbers and must be organised. Fifteen years ago the accepted view was that we didn't need to organise people like cooks and bottle washers and home helps and cleaners. They weren't real trade unionists because they weren't real people. Real people were white, skilled, male working class. Thankfully that can't be said any more (at least not openly). The work I have tried to do has been about enabling people to participate rather than merely be represented. By participating they change, the process changes, and the trade union movement changes.

NUPE in Northern Ireland is a region which now has 40 per cent more members than when Thatcher came to power. That wasn't easy to achieve. To the majority of our members NUPE is regarded within their communities as somewhere to turn if there's trouble with a local issue, not just a work-based issue. The union is regarded as a social force. I believe that reflects women's way of not separating or fragmenting issues.

Women in Northern Ireland are as politicised as women in Britain, but less likely to be involved in the political process or political parties. The characteristic of women in Northern Ireland is rather to be highly involved in community organisations. Most women here face major problems of social and economic deprivation but there are also special problems because of the political situation. On top of the other struggles of daily life, some women who live in nationalist or republican areas face the burden of being virtually single parent families; their husbands, sons or daughters may be in prison as a result of the troubles. If a member of the family is doing twenty years inside then so are the women outside.

The same would be true for some Protestant women but there would also be a different emphasis. Many of them would face the anxiety of their husbands being in the security forces, the police or UDR and it is the women who have to live with the consequences of much of the stress which might display itself as their men having drink problems or huge gambling problems or huge debt problems. The women don't necessarily see all the money but they do have to cope with the consequences.

The Protestant culture produces a more passive acceptance of the system but there are signs that that is beginning to change. The Catholic culture produces a challenge to the system. I'm not talking about the national question. It takes much longer to break the passivity of Protestants on issues than it would Catholics. Women live in a culture where both are outside the system. Catholic women might more readily react to issues of inequality and injustice. Protestant women may be slower to react but that's changing. Neither are really consulted by the men of politics, nationalist or unionist.

In some places like Derry there is a strong identity and although it can be very enclosed and uncomfortable for a woman trying to transform her view of herself, it can also be very supportive. In areas where there is generational unemployment and people are very damaged by such problems women know that it is not the people themselves who are the problem. Women are the core of such communities.

I would contrast that with much of the south east of England where unemployment is hitting hard with little culture of support. In a town like Derry, with its dispossession and its 40 per cent unemployment, people feel and understand marginalisation but they are also proud of their identity. They love the place, the way of life. It's one of the most vibrant cities in Ireland. The ideas are flowing, the literature is flowing, the music's flowing and this is a strong community culture. It is a largely Catholic town which is trying to accept and include the Protestant minority in that culture.

I come from a Loyalist background. I left home at sixteen because of family circumstances. I worked in the Civil Service just to get a job and did O and A levels at night. I then went to university, not as a form of developing my intellect, but as an escape. I met my husband in a bar in the Earls Court Road in London. He comes from a Catholic working-class background, a background I had no contact with during my early years and in my teens. Marrying caused initial problems for both our families and some of the scars are still there. My husband was a founder member of the Derry Labour Party and when we returned to Derry we became very involved with the civil rights movement.

I worked as a social worker for a short period and was extremely dissatisfied with the job. I suppose it was what I saw there which helped to transform me. There was another war going on besides the emerging war between the IRA and the government. It was the absolute humiliation of very poor working-class people who were not being treated as badly as Afro-Americans in the southern States but had the same relationship with the establishment. They were treated as if they were animals and did not have rights. That particularly hit the women because they had a double burden. They were the ones who had to hassle for the family allowance, who had to deal with the housing authorities – and if you were a

Catholic from Ballymurphy, you started at the bottom of the queue. They were told things like 'You've got a house but you should be living in an orange box.' I saw children with spina bifida who couldn't get treatment.

The women had to take the hassle of living with huge bureaucracies, dealing with them and dealing with the problems of husbands who couldn't get a job. If the husband couldn't handle things it was often taken out on the wife. I've seen the tragedy on too many women's faces and it was that war I was reacting to, not the other one. I later learned it was necessary to deal with both.

Eventually the women started coming to us for advice. To me – a young Protestant in Ballymurphy in the middle of a war in people's private lives and a war on the street with guns! These women were geniuses as far as I was concerned, even though I was meant to be the counsellor. I gave them money, vouchers, anything I could. They were the ones who knew how to struggle and survive. Then the authorities closed our office. We refused to go and they sacked us but we kept coming into work. So they withdrew the sackings but said the office must still close. Somebody said I should join a union so I became a NUPE shop steward.

Then I became pregnant. I lost my baby largely because of circumstances in the area – because of illness not because of the troubles. I was so ill that I couldn't work for a while and did part-time work with the union.

I became interested in organising the people I had worked for, and applied for a fulltime NUPE job in spite of being told that I wouldn't get it because I was a woman. I went along for the interview without telling them I was now five months pregnant. When they asked me what I would do if I had children I said, 'With the help of the British Labour Party and the trade union movement, if it puts its money where its mouth is I'll have no problem.' So they asked me how I would handle coming home from a rough dock meeting late at night to which I replied, 'You should make it a condition of service that every NUPE officer drives through Belfast at lunchtime.' I got the job and wrote back that I would accept it in a year's time when my baby would hopefully be six months old. It was International Women's Year, 1975, so they couldn't say no. I had to have 1,200 members within six months on the books in Northern Ireland or I would be transferred. That condition has never been set for any other officer before or since and I did it. Thankfully things are changing.

I was the first woman officer in the union, the first woman from the North ever elected to the Executive Council of Irish Congress, the first woman elected on to the regional TUC. All those firsts can disguise the struggle and anguish of getting there and being there. 'Firsts' aren't important if a woman doesn't make a real effort to make sure that there are second, third and fourth women and so on.

I'm interested in women taking power, but I'm more interested in them redefining it as a way of challenging inequality in relationships and in society. Three or four hundred women taking on a bad boss is much more effective than taking him to court.

I am struggling to understand where post-feminism or 'the backlash' fits into any of this. The idea that it has 'all gone too far' is laughable in terms of the women I represent. I understand the arguments and I have talked to American women about the backlash there. I presume it's to do with women becoming visible. And that takes us to the discussion of power. Where and how do women hold power? We may hold positions, but we should never confuse that with holding power. How are women using power? Are we redefining it by opening up new processes? Are we about change rather than exchange?

The viciousness of the backlash to visibility alone should warn us of the depths of resistance to our struggle to influence and control our own destiny.

MARGERET FORSTER

'Women are right to want everything now'

Margaret Forster is a writer whose work includes Significant Sisters *which traces the history of the feminist movement.*

Nobody is quite sure what the word feminism means. When you say to someone: 'Are you a feminist?' you still get that indignant reply 'Certainly not', as though you have asked them something awful. Then you have to explain that you are a feminist because, contrary to what people think, feminism to you simply means that you shouldn't be prevented from doing anything by reason of your gender. You can be prevented for lots of other reasons – like lack of strength so you can't be a labourer or something like that – but not because of your gender.

But why hasn't it succeeded more than it has done? And why do we have to keep fighting the same battles? Every time people think the battle is won, like getting the vote or more protective legislation in the workplace, there is always something else and you have got to start again with the next generation. As a movement it just hasn't grown in a logical way. It is not like socialism; you can't join a party and get a card and belong. Only when there is some particular issue to march for does it emerge again.

I don't know why we have never had a separate feminist party. Even at the height of the nineteenth-century struggles no one suggested that we should have a feminist party and I think it is because the vast majority of women are anti joining things. That is why we don't have more women MPs in Parliament. I have always been fascinated by the fact that women like me who care, who have some ideas, who are articulate, who have got the financial means, don't try to become MPs. It isn't a good enough answer to say because we are domesticated and our interior life in the house is more important than anything that lies outside. I could and would have given that as the answer years ago because somehow I never wanted to leave my nice, cosy domestic set-up – my vision was sort of stuck at the door of the house – but when you get to fifty all that is different. I now have the time to do what I want to do and to be political in a way that is necessary. But still I don't do it and that seems to me to be a feminist problem. With educated women like me all that energy that has been used over the years on other things is suddenly freed and could theoretically be put to another use and it is tragic that women like myself are so inactive in that way. What keeps us back from throwing ourselves into the public arena? I admire all the women who do tremendously. But I went to Glenda Jackson's meetings in our constituency before the election and listened to her talk and so on, and after about half an hour I thought: 'I couldn't stand this – this would drive me potty – having to slog it out in this way.' I couldn't get home quick enough, and I feel the same way every time I attempt to go to the local Labour Party meetings (which I only do out of shame when it is really necessary).

It could be the inability on my part to be a team worker, or that I don't have the patience, but I think it is more than that and I think it is the reason why most women will not participate politically. History shows that all the women who started movements, even the suffragettes, only banded together to work for specific goals and when – and I don't wish to denigrate – their relatively small goal was achieved, their personal involvement was finished, over. My work on the feminist movement also showed me that women tended to participate because something personal happened to them. Very few of them had the breadth to see that all the issues were interconnected and one was no good without the other. They were very single-minded which was what made them successful, but it also made them a bit blinkered. If you were Emily Davies* and couldn't get the education you most passionately wanted, you became so angry that you took the system on. If you were Josephine Butler** and went to work with the prostitutes in Liverpool, you saw how awful it was that they became prostitutes for economic reasons and you got a sense of mission. I think Helena Kennedy is a modern feminist heroine – what she is doing for these women in prison who have killed their husbands is not just real practical help, it is becoming a little bit of a movement against those dreadful male judges and QCs and, unlike some feminists who militate against themselves because of their manner, she is warm and witty with a razor-sharp brain. We need more people like her to come up front.

I keep thinking maybe one day I'll get my sense of mission. But I think I could already have been motivated by a couple of issues that could have been the spark, but they haven't sparked me and I sit here all the time feeling ashamed, and thinking why don't I do something, but I never do. Then I let myself off the hook by thinking, well I can write. But it isn't really a good enough answer.

A lot of women's reluctance to get involved goes back to conditioning and, if I had grown up with a father who was even remotely political, I might have been different. So many women who are active in the Labour Party, particularly working-class women, had families with a father – sometimes a mother, but more often a father – who belonged to a trade union or the local party. They were involved from a very early age and they heard things talked about and they understood what they were fighting for. But the majority of working-class girls, from homes like mine where parents thought

---

* Emily Davies was a feminist education reformer who founded Girton College, Cambridge.

** Josephine Butler campaigned against nineteenth-century sex legislation, such as the Contagious Diseases Act, which illustrated the complex Victorian attitudes towards women and sexuality.

politics were nothing whatsoever to do with them, were not motivated. My father was the typical working-class man. He worked in a factory as a fitter and hated the unions because their activities meant the risk of going on strike and he was too scared to cross the picket line and didn't want to be unemployed again. When I was twelve or thirteen and beginning to learn about these things, we started having violent arguments in which I would try and argue that the trade unions were fighting for him. He had left school at thirteen, was not self-educated (he never read), and that is the climate in which I was brought up. It wasn't exactly apathy, it was: 'The wealthy are on the other side of the fence and there is nothing that could be done about it.' So I was conditioned to accept my lot and try not to change anything.

When I was about eleven and was a witness to an accident in the street and very eager to give evidence, my father went mad because he was terrified of me getting involved. Even going down to the education office to sign papers for my grant for Oxford practically meant my mother putting a gun at his head because of his terror of officialdom and desire to conform. He was furious when I joined the Labour Party. He would rather I had been a Tory, and would say things like: 'I voted Labour once in 1945 and they did nowt for me,' so I think he has voted Tory ever since and certainly he loved Margaret Thatcher. The whole of the council estate I lived on was like that and it wasn't until I got to Oxford that I met any different kinds of people, the sort of working-class people who are brought up in a completely different tradition and it was good for me because I saw that something could be done about these issues.

This kind of conditioning is harder for women to overcome than men because in a way their biological programme and history also acts as a brake. I actually believe very strongly in that, even though I know most modern feminists don't. I think when you have your first child something changes; it did in me, and everything is secondary to the child. By the time you have had two or three they are always put first and it amazes me to think that some women have managed to step out of that into the public arena. I know if I had wanted to be something else I could never have managed it. I think women are right to want everything now – that is one of the great breakthroughs – and I don't think there is any need to do it the way I did it, but my conditioning got in the way.

I got married in 1960 and had the first child in 1964 and was still teaching then, although I immediately dropped it when my first novel was published. By the time I had three children, I was writing all the time but I would have been horrified at the idea of getting any woman to work in the house which seemed a terrible betrayal. Even worse was to have anyone look after your children – what possible excuse could there be for that? It was stupid, but that is how I felt. So I was doing everything and having to be very disciplined in order to work. With the first two children I wrote only three nights a week and at the weekend when Hunter, my husband, would take them out. Then by the time Flora was born – she was more than six years younger – I would write while the other two were at school and she was asleep. It was a nightmare. Why did I do it? Because I felt I should. Because I felt that it was wrong to exploit people to clean your house and all that. I also think there is a physical reaction to leaving a baby. I can remember leaving our first daughter for the first time when she was about five months and feeling absolutely physically panicky. I felt I had left part of myself behind and that is a common experience. Perhaps it's easier if you leave the baby with your mother or your sister, which still goes on in Carlisle where we are from, but not down here. I was also afraid of the burden of relationships. I can't stand people in the house – I like the house to be mine for at least half of the day and couldn't bear the idea of having to make friends with someone who cleaned it or who looked after the children. I knew I would never have been able to literally have them clocking in and clocking out. But I regret it looking back and if women are going to have it all – which I am all for – then they should have good help and there should be more flexibility on the part of the employers.

But I actually liked being a housewife and a mother and I was not bored. I loved cleaning and domesticity and being out with the children. I liked it all. Most women like two out of the three. Sometimes just one out of the three. They know if they stayed at home with the children they would go stark raving mad but I didn't. I don't think I could have coped if I had gone out to work.

In spite of the fact that we are 150 years on, there are remarkable similarities between women, which cross class, because the biological problems are exactly the same. You have your first child and suddenly everything changes; it doesn't matter whether you are rich or poor, your feelings towards a child remain a constant brake, the question of where your allegiance is going at every challenge remains a brake, the fact that you worry all the time about these creatures you've given birth to. It makes you less sharp, less aware of everything outside your domestic set-up, and it affects ambition in most women, and they never rise above it. They are not going to do that because of the children. The really valuable feminists are the ones who don't have children. It is very sad but true. Women can work with lovers, working together can even make them more ambitious – but not with the children. I do believe that women are split in a way that men aren't after children are born. Most men still see the children as being the wife's responsibility, no matter how much they care.

My children think I have never worked. If I had gone off with my little briefcase, power dressed, it would have been easier for them to understand. My son's friends say I can't be a feminist because when they have been staying here they see me getting up at about seven, taking Hunter a cup of coffee and the newspaper, putting his radio on and opening the curtains, then he stays there like Louis XIV till about 8.30 and then slowly gets up. I always tell them that if I had to do this, it would be wrong, but I *choose* to do it and that amazes them. Even these very educated youths think that feminism means that you are all out for yourself. The girls are terrific though, they don't stand for anything. When they are put to the test they come out exactly how you would want them to – the result of being in mixed sixth forms at school which gives girls a huge social advantage. They can be quite terrifying really. I'm still always anxious to be a good girl – my home conditioning again – and do things the right way, but my children's generation don't care about that. They won't put up with anything they disagree with.

But most of them are not politically active and some of them have this idea that to be a feminist you have to be butch and un-attractive in dungarees and they don't want to be like that. They don't see that feminism is a good set of ideas which are for the benefit of men too and that any man married to a feminist is lucky and he is usually a feminist himself. Some of the best feminists have been men, and individual movements, like Josephine Butler's, would have never succeeded if it hadn't been for the men. She couldn't go into the brothels – but the men did and gathered the evidence and it was a man who published it at great cost to himself.

© Regine Koerner

SHAWN SLOVO

'You can't avoid a sense of guilt as a white South African'

Shawn Slovo is a screenwriter whose work includes the film A World Apart *which was based on her early life. She grew up in South Africa where her parents, Joe Slovo and Ruth First, were anti-apartheid activists. Her mother was one of the first women to be detained under the South African ninety-day detention laws in the early sixties and was assassinated in 1982.*

I lived in Johannesburg for the first thirteen years of my life and have very happy memories of South Africa. It was a fantastic country for a child to grow up in. We had space, beautiful weather and the people, both black and white, are very warm. We were brought up by nannies and maids and had a very close relationship with them. As a result of my parents' political involvement in the anti-apartheid struggle, we came into exile in Britain in 1963. It would have been impossible to stay in South Africa as the leadership of the anti-apartheid movement was either being forced into exile or imprisoned and it was a low point in the history of the ANC.

I always wanted to go into the film industry, partly because I wanted to combine my love of films with writing, but also because I wanted to be in an area that was completely different to my parents. What could be more of a contrast to the South African struggle than working for Hollywood and being involved in that fantasy world? I worked in the States until my mother, who had since returned to Africa to live in Mozambique, was assassinated in 1982. That was a kind of watershed for me and I came back here to the National Film School. Her death brought all sorts of things into focus and I felt that this was the time to start writing, which was what I had always wanted to do.

I combined my ambition to write with trying to come to terms with what had happened to my mother and wrote the script that eventually became *A World Apart*. She was a very complicated woman and there was a lot of unresolved business between us which is really what the film was about. Towards the end of her life, we were both beginning to be able to talk about the past differently and I had started to go to therapy. She was very responsive to that, and anyway was changing, getting older, feeling more secure in a way. Being back in Africa, living and working in Mozambique, she seemed happier than she had been in the years of exile.

When we were growing up, she had been the breadwinner because my father had escaped South Africa and life imprisonment after the Rivonia trials by a fluke coincidence: he happened to be out of the country when Mandela, Sisulu et al were arrested. His commitment intensified, and there was never any doubt in his mind about how he would spend the rest of his life. I suppose I was put off politics because I felt excluded. They tried to give us as normal an upbringing as possible but they were quite self-absorbed. They were in their late-twenties, early-thirties and were having the most fantastically exciting time. There was a lot of subterfuge, conspiracy, meeting on street corners, invisible ink and god knows what else. More importantly, there was a sense of optimism. Joe now says that, had they known in the 1950s what the course of the South African struggle would be, they would have thought twice about having a family. The country is in an incredible mess, there are huge problems and will be for generations. But at least the change has started.

I don't think you can avoid a sense of guilt as a white, South African, middle-class person, and that is the most difficult thing to live with. You try to ignore it and live in exclusive white suburbs and build huge high walls to keep everyone out. It is like a fortress, and how can that not affect the way you live, the way you think about things and relate to other people? Everyone out there has this guilt from being brought up very closely by a black woman which creates a real, close bond which, as you become aware of the society and the rules of the society you live in, you have to deny. What is more, in order to look after you, she has to forego looking after her own family. Imagine what sorrow she carries around with her. In spite of my feelings about what my parents did and the effect it had on me, I'm extremely proud of the choices that they made.

The process of making a film about my own life was very cathartic, but hard. Life is not film and it took a lot of work to get over the anger and pain and refine it until I could look at the characters as separate from me and my family. I worked it through in the writing and by the time it got to the shooting stage it was a story that was based on my own experience and was not really recognisable as mine.

There is no film industry in this country to speak of, and no financial or tax incentives for investors in film production. There's fantastic talent here: writers, directors, actors, but we're let down badly by the producers. There's no confidence, no imagination, no vision, at least in feature film production. I've been lucky to be able to stay here and make a living, employed mainly by Hollywood. It's lonely, not being part of a film community, but I just don't think it would be healthy to live in California, for a writer. It's a narrow world view and it shows in the way you begin to write. And there's too much preoccupation with the business, and with the gossip of the business. It's very seductive.

I'm not political but the preoccupations I have in my work, and the kinds of stories I gravitate to and want to tell, reflect a loathing of injustice. I think it's when I write best.

Jane Bown

YVONNE ROBERTS

'Short-change women and you short-change society'

Yvonne Roberts is a feminist writer and journalist. She was one of the original team on London Weekend's Weekend World *and was more recently editor of the* Observer *living pages. Her last book,* Mad about Women *argued that the feminist movement needs a new agenda.*

I think women have been far too polite for too long. Twenty-five years after the second wave of feminism, we're still saying 'Please' and 'Thank you' for the most minimal changes. A few companies make fairly empty promises as part of Opportunity 2000 and women are supposed to express enormous gratitude – for what? For nothing, except the fact that a few firms have got cheap publicity at the price of women's genuine progress. If women don't make a stand now, the future promises short-term contracts, permanent casualisation, no pension schemes, no maternity leave, no career breaks.

Ten million women have entered the work-force since the sixties. Two thirds of mothers hold down jobs – but the workplace still operates as if nobody has a family; nobody bears children; everyone wants to be a workaholic. Such attitudes aren't just discriminatory, they affect profits adversely too. Research shows that treating women fairly in the workplace is also highly cost-effective. Short-change women and you short-change society.

Feminism in the sixties happened in a decade of optimism. It focussed on the view that women were victims and second class citizens, but then we also felt something could be done. Now, such ideas also bring with them a sense of passivity and hopelessness. So, I believe that however hard it is for many, it's time that we got off our bums, stopped being 'victims', acknowledged responsibility for ourselves – and gave the establishment hell.

The 'nice' women in the suffragette movement did precisely that. They blew up postboxes; smashed shop windows; chained themselves to railings; ran their own newspaper; mobilised on an extraordinary scale – and persuaded thousands that nice women don't achieve nearly as much as bad women do. They also won the vote.

In the nineties, we are faced with too few rights for part-time workers; unequal pay; poor maternity leave; almost no parental leave; totally inadequate provisions in social security; no national subsidised childcare and 'femocrat' organisations such as the Equal Opportunities Commission who rely too much on government grants to rock the boat with the real vigour that's required now.

Direct action today would have to be different from the form it took seventy-five years ago. It needs humour and good marketing. It isn't a whingers' charter but about women who don't want to put up with any more lip-service. It needs to be as much about persuading women that they can organise and achieve change as it is about telling society that women – millions of them – have had enough of being marginalised and rendered invisible.

Out of small protests, major catalysts are born. Look at the poll tax protest and the women against pit closures and the campaigns in the USA against changes in abortion legislation.

We also need to exploit the changes in the media. A female perspective is absent in most of the press – except in the ghetto of the women's pages. But now women are earning money, the press is being forced to take us more seriously. We even have a handful of women leader writers and a couple of female columnists who are allowed to stray from sexual politics into political commentary, where grown-up men have long been allowed to play.

If a campaign of direct action is planned well enough and sold hard, and uses, for instance, some of the tactics employed by campaigns such as Comic Relief, it will revamp feminism's image as well as force the media to take issues such as part-time workers' rights on board in a more sustained way. The press will, of course, try to prove that the campaign is run by heavily moustached types with no sense of humour, no libido and no public support. But we could have a lot of fun proving otherwise.

At times when I was publicising my book, I was termed in the press 'the acceptable face of feminism'. I think it was meant to be a compliment, but I didn't regard it as such. If I'm 'acceptable', I'm harmless, easily accommodated into the mainstream of society. And for me, and many like me, it's partly precisely because we've been too accommodating that society has failed to adjust speedily enough.

Women have one muscle that they've failed to exercise much – and that's their collective muscle. Even if only a fraction of over 25 million women stand together and get tough, it could begin a chain reaction.

Many of the women of the sixties, like me, have reached middle age. We have daughters and sons whom we want to live in a decent, more balanced, fairer society. We're getting a second wind and we don't have time to wait for another fifty years of slow reform during which the Labour Party or the trade union movement or the CBI may or may not give women another small pat on the head. Women are an integral part of any strategy to transform Britain from a nineteenth-century society into a community equipped to deal with the twenty-first-century world. Those who don't understand that, don't deserve to govern.

The first step is for us to re-find our voices. If women don't tell society what they require to become much vaunted active citizens – and if we don't explain clearly what we'll do if such demands are ignore – nobody else is going to do it for us.

VALERIE AMOS

'If I could have three wishes'

Valerie Amos is the chief executive of the Equal Opportunities Commission. She was born in Guyana and came to this country in the sixties with her parents, who were both teachers. Her career has also spanned senior management posts in local government.

I came to this country from Guyana when I was nine, and was the first black girl to go to the girl's technical high school near where we lived in Kent – my sister was the second. Looking back, I don't think I felt odd being the only black child in a white school. I don't recall any overt racism, but I think it was probably quite an isolating experience. I was very quiet and academic and I think I just got stuck into the work. There was curiosity though and when the school choir used to go and sing in old people's homes at Christmas, the residents would always touch my skin and hair because I was probably the first black person they had ever seen.

Both my parents were teachers. I was brought up in an environment where education was important and grew up with a passionate interest in social and public policy. We always talked politics at home and were encouraged to argue and debate, to question and challenge, even if it meant challenging someone in authority. When we first went to primary school, for example, I wasn't given a reading test and was automatically put in the bottom class. But when my mother insisted they test me, I was put in the top class.

My sister then came home in a rage because, in a geography class, someone said she came from Africa and lived in a mud hut. My parents sent her back with photographs to show that Guyana wasn't Africa, that we did not live in mud huts and told her to tell her teachers that Africa was a continent, not a country.

My parents never let us forget we were black, that being black carried with it certain responsibilities and that we didn't have to take any racism or snide comments. Going to Warwick University to read sociology was a natural extension of that environment – I wanted to go there because they had courses in the sociology of race relations and the sociology of women's issues.

By the time I left university with all the confidence of youth, I felt I could change the world, but I didn't know quite how. I went to Birmingham to do an MA in contemporary cultural studies, because I wanted to work with Stuart Hall who was one of the leading figures in studying race and cultural issues. After that I felt pulled in two different directions – between the world of work and academia. By that time I was involved in a whole range of community activities in Birmingham, like helping to set up a black women's group, and I had worked as a community education officer for a year in Handsworth. I went back to university, to East Anglia, to do a research project looking at the transition from school to work for black girls. I did my research in Birmingham, and as part of a community project took a group of young black people back to Jamaica to explore how they felt about their Caribbean roots.

I had experience of local authorities from the outside because of my academic work and my community work and I decided to take a job as a race adviser in the London Borough of Lambeth, which was a really good introduction to local government, because I was in a management team working at a high level, but in an advisory capacity. Then I went to Camden as a women's adviser, then to Hackney Council to be head of training and then head of management services. My job was to look at organisational efficiency, while trying to improve service delivery and harness the commitment of the staff in a climate of public expenditure cuts. Management services was still a male-dominated area of local government and not many women had made it to such a post. When the job at the Commission came up I did wonder about going back to managing equal opportunities, but this is a key national organisation, with a lot of influence, so I took the job as chief executive and came here at thirty-five.

I think there are all sorts of things that the EOC can do and is doing to get the public to understand our role better. There are enormous constraints on an organisation like this. We are publicly funded, publicly accountable and everybody has the right to complain or praise or make a comment about our work. Any organisation that has such an enormous constituency, with differing interests, is always going to find it difficult to balance all those interests. On the one hand we have women saying we are not radical enough, even though there is no homogeneity between women and women's organisations about what they expect from us. On the other hand we have to be concerned with equal treatment between women and men – we are not concerned solely to protect the interests of women – and we get a lot of complaints from men.

While we can demonstrate through our research that the major impact of sex discrimination – for example in terms of pay, part-time work and social security – is on women, the Commission still has a role in terms of balancing those interests and not losing support from other sections of the public. It is quite a difficult balancing act and is probably one of the most challenging aspects of managing the EOC.

We have made huge strides in a number of areas. After arguing long and hard over issues around discrimination in taxation, there have finally been changes to the law. We would also say that, although the pay gap isn't narrowing fast enough, it has narrowed a little bit according to the official government figures and is now around 21 per cent, but if you look at non-manual earnings the gap is 33 per cent. A lot of that has to do with the campaigning from the EOC, although we have a lot of work still to do. The legislation surrounding equal pay and equal value is far too complicated. As it stands now, you always have to have a comparator for equal treatment cases but because we have a highly sex-segregated work-force, that's often difficult to find, but if you don't have a comparator it is very difficult to bring a case in the first place. On average a case takes seventeen months to get to court, but there are cases that take much much longer – up to seven or eight years, by which time people have given up, or changed jobs and the importance of the issue has faded away.

I think we would also point to our work to get equality in pensions as being very much at the forefront of pushing for change, and our work in trying to integrate some of the race and sex discrimination issues in employment, especially among low-paid women, has been important, although we have been particularly hampered in that by the lack of statistical evidence to back up what we know is happening. Fifty percent of home workers are black women – and home workers are a particularly large section of the low paid. We have done a lot of work in the European arena and have used our law enforcement powers in a very strategic way to take cases to the European Court, which will have an influence on domestic legislation.

There has been progress for women, but only certain things are highlighted by the media, like getting women into top jobs. They are only a tiny proportion of women though and, while it is important to get them into influential positions in management, their success doesn't necessarily touch the lives of the majority of women. Nearly half of working women work part-time. The majority work in jobs that are low paid, not necessarily protected, where the working environment is extremely difficult, where there is increasing fragmentation of collective bargaining and increasing casualisation of the work-force. The changes in the public sector, in terms of the contracting out of services, have also had a disproportionate impact on women, who are concentrated in jobs like catering and cleaning.

To the media a lot of these issues are not seen as issues of equal opportunities, and I think the EOC has to demonstrate that it has an interest way beyond just getting women into senior management positions. We are about trying to bring about fundamental changes in society that will have an impact on those women.

The argument put back to us is that the changes we want to see will be a burden on management and industry and will make Britain less competitive. But we would argue that European countries with high cost, highly skilled, highly motivated workforces create a 'quality scenario' as opposed to what we call the 'cost-cutting' scenario, where everything is about bargain basement prices and low pay. European comparisons are also useful in terms of highlighting our poor infrastructure. We have one of the worst records in terms of childcare provision and we don't compare well in terms of parental leave. It is important that policy makers and members of the public know that it is done in a different way elsewhere.

We are aware that people feel very threatened at the moment because of the recession, so it is a bad time to be making arguments about equality and training because people are worried about simply getting or keeping a job. But I think it is an argument which we have to continue to make. It is getting harder for women to make themselves heard because they traditionally organise through their communities, but there has been a squeeze on community organisations because of public expenditure cuts and local authorities taking funding away from voluntary organisations. Economic changes mean people have had to concentrate very much on themselves, and women bear a lot of responsibility for holding families together. I feel more optimistic about younger women, who I think have grown up with a sense of feeling they have certain rights. I think a lot of them will get some serious shocks once they get out in the world but maybe those shocks will generate some action.

We are about to reprioritise education now that the changes of the Education Act are becoming clearer. We can now look and see whether the national curriculum is delivering equality and the effect of the local management of schools on equal opportunities. A lot of the very good equal opportunities work that had been done through local authorities is now disappearing, because they have much less of a role in individual schools. A lot of authorities no longer have equal opportunities advisers and sometimes it does feel as if we could be going backwards. We can't influence every school, but we have to find the most strategic ways of making change. We have to find a way of influencing without all the resources of the Commission being committed to one issue.

If I could have three wishes, the first would be to see one law for equal pay and sex discrimination, simplified so equal pay could be delivered. The second would be to see much stronger monitoring of employers, in both the public and private sector, along the lines of the Fair Employment Commission in Northern Ireland, which has the right, backed up by law, to get information from organisations and make recommendations about what they should do to bring about equality. Thirdly I would like to see women themselves organising more and recognising that they are a force and a power – and using that to best effect.

MAD ABOUT WOMEN
Can There Ever Be Fair Play Between The Sexes?
Yvonne Roberts

Are men now second class citizens? Do they have fresh reason in the 1990s for being mad about women? British journalist Yvonne Roberts challenges writers such as Neil Lyndon who argue that feminism has poisoned relations between the sexes, emasculated men and stolen their children.

She takes up where Susan Faludi's *Backlash* left off and argues with passion and wit that while feminism has had setbacks, some self-inflicted, it remains *the* major transforming force of the century.

Drawing on interviews throughout Britain, she presses for a new alliance between women and with men, and a re-vitalised agenda: an agenda that challenges head-on a society which tramples on the poor and disenfranchised and equates 'success' with workaholism and female liberation with working a sixteen-hour day.

THE HEART OF THE RACE
Black Women's Lives in Britain

Edited by Beverley Bryan, Stelle Dadzie and Suzanne Scaffe

'A balanced tribute to the undefeated creativity, resilience and resourcefulness of Black women in Britain today' – *Margaret Busby, New Society*

WINNER OF THE MARTIN LUTHER KING MEMORIAL PRIZE (1985)

'Our aim has been to tell it as we know it, placing our story within its history at the heart of our race, and using our own voices and lives to document the day-to-day realities of Afro-Caribbean women in Britain over the past forty years.'

The Heart of the Race powerfully records what life is like for Black women in Britain: grandmothers drawn to the promise of the 'mother country' in the 1950s talk of a different reality; young girls describe how their aspirations at school are largely ignored; working women tell of their commitments to families, jobs, communities. With clarity and determination, these Afro-Caribbean women discuss their treatment by the Welfare State, their housing situations, their health, their self-images – and their confrontation with the racism they encounter all too often. Here too is Black women's celebration of their culture and their struggle to create a new social order in this country.

REFUSING HOLY ORDERS
Women and Fundamentalism in Britain

Edited by Gita Sahgal and Nira Yuval-Davis

From the Rushdie affair to attacks on abortion clinics, from the setting up of Muslim schools for girls to domestic violence within Asian communities; all reflect how religious fundamentalism is on the rise. This pioneering collection looks at the particular ways in which women affect and are affected by these movements – Christian, Jewish, Muslim, Hindu – in Britain. For, in the instability of the '90s, dogmatic religious beliefs call for a return to traditional values – particularly to the control of women within the patriarchal family. Identity, gender roles within the family and wider communities, attitudes towards contraception, and women's work – all become issues of control – and arenas of resistance.

The contributors are Yasmin Ali, Elaine Foster, Saeeda Khanum, Sara Maitland, Maryam Poya, Ann Rossiter and the book's editors.

ONE HAND TIED BEHIND US
The Rise of the Women's Suffrage Movement

Jill Liddington and Jill Norris

'A brilliant and original contribution to the history of female suffrage' – *The Times*

The north of England was the cradle of the suffrage movement: here women worked long hours in factories and mills, struggled against poverty and hardship at home, and, at the turn of the century, fought not only for the vote but for a wide range of women's rights. These radical suffragists, amongst them remarkable women like Selina Cooper and Ada Nield Chew, called for equal pay, birth control and child allowances. They took their message to women at the factory gate and the cottage door, to the Co-operative Guilds and trade union branches.

One Hand Tied Behind Us, using much unpublished material and interviews with the last surviving descendants of these suffragists, creates a vivid and moving portrait of strong women who, over seventy years ago, envisaged freedoms for which we are still fighting today.

THE SUFRAGETTE MOVEMENT

Sylvia Pankhurst
Preface by Dr Richard Pankhurst

'What Sylvia communicates is . . . a feeling of what it was like
to live through that struggle . . . a full and very readable
memoir' – *Margaret Walters, New Society*

The Suffragette Movement is unique, for it is the only major history
of the fight for the vote to be written by one of the movement's
central participants. It chronicles the progress of the struggle
which began in the late nineteenth century and continued until
after the First World War, a triumph of courage and
determination. It also covers many aspects of the wider campaign
for women's rights at the beginning of the twentieth century, and
includes Sylvia Pankhurst's classic account of her attempt to
organize working women in the East End of London.

As well as being an important primary source for the study of the
period, *The Suffragette Movement* is a fascinating memoir of the
Pankhursts, one of the most extraordinary British political families
of the last hundred years.

ROUND ABOUT A POUND A WEEK
Maud Pember Reeves

'Highly readable' – *Naomi Hutchison*

'A justly celebrated classic' – *David Rubinstein*

From 1909 to 1913, undaunted by the proposition that a 'bi-weekly visit to Lambeth is like a plunge into Hades', the Fabian Women's Group recorded the daily budgets of thirty families in Lambeth living on about a pound a week. In 1913 they published this record in *Round About a Pound a Week*, a rare and vivid portrait of the daily life of working people.

We learn about family life, births, marriages and deaths; of grinding work carried out on a diet of little more than bread, jam and margarine. We learn how they coped with damp, vermin and bedbugs – how they slept: four to a bed, in banana crates – how they washed, cooked, cleaned, scrimped for furniture and clothes, saved for the all too frequent burials . . .

With a vivid and compassionate eye *Round About a Pound a Week* captures, as no camera could, the everyday life of seventy years ago. Historically unique, and more, a moving and evocative human document.

LIFE AS WE HAVE KNOWN IT
By Co-operative Working Women

Edited by Margaret Llewelyn Davis

'It has all the inspirational quality Virginia Woolf found in it nearly fifty years ago' – *The Times*

'. . . one looked back into the past of the women who stood there; into the four-roomed houses of miners, into the homes of small shopkeepers and agricultural labourers, into the fields and factories of fifty or sixty years ago . . .'
Virginia Woolf

Life As We Have Known It, first published at the Hogarth Press in 1931, is a classic, first-hand record of the lives of working women. They tell of their childhoods – growing up in poverty and want; of work – begun in most cases when still children; of domestic service, work in factories and fields; of family life – husbands often old and ill before their time, childbirth, marriage, death.

The remarkable women who wrote this book were members of the Women's Co-operative Guild, founded in 1883, a powerful agent in the education of working women. The experiences and aspirations recounted here are, as Virginia Woolf says, a witness to the 'extraordinary vitality of the human spirit'.